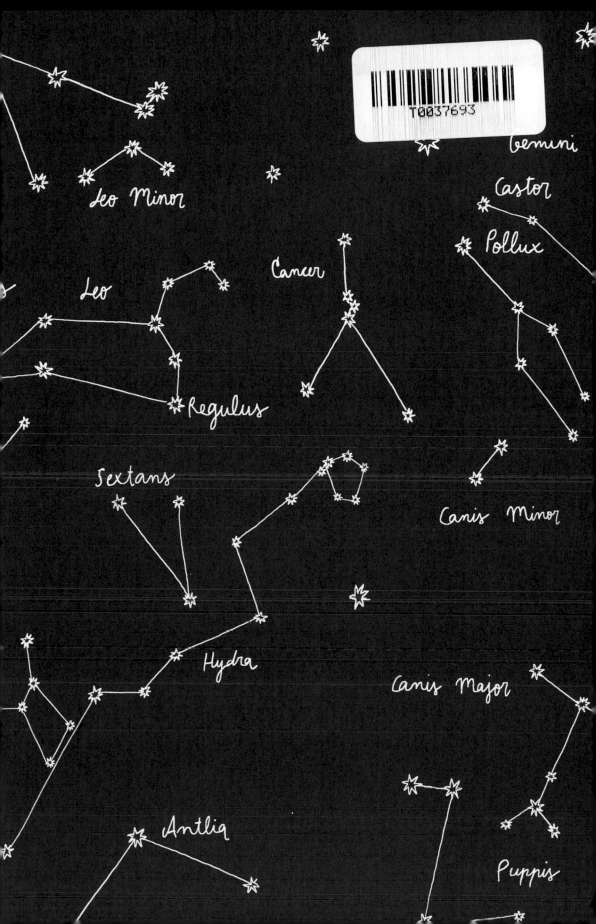

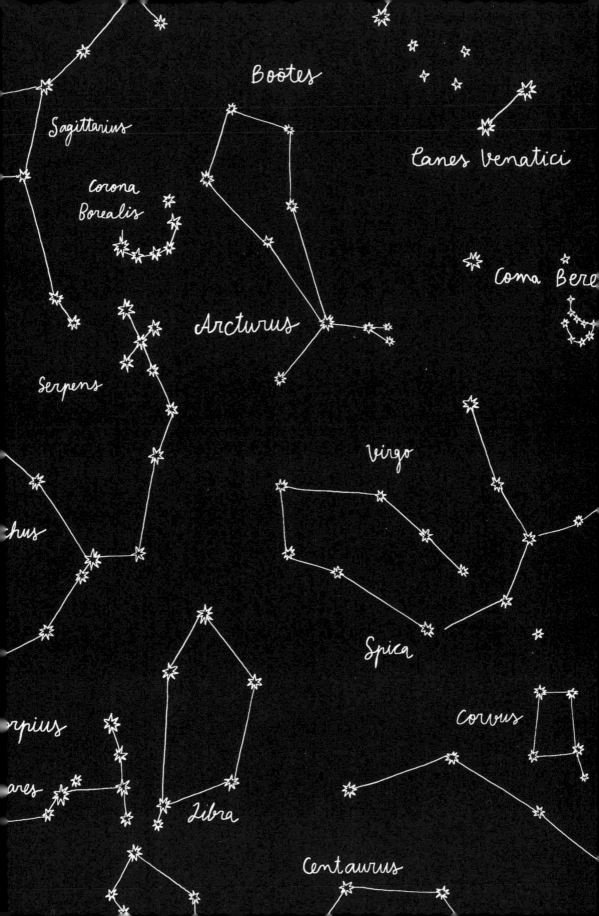

SIGNS *of the* ZODIAC

SIGNS *of the* ZODIAC

A MODERN GUIDE TO THE
AGE-OLD WISDOM OF THE STARS

Carlota Santos

Artisan | New York

Library of Congress Cataloging-in-Publication Data

Names: Santos, Carlota, author.
Title: Signs of the zodiac : a modern guide to the age-old wisdom of the stars / Carlota Santos.
Description: New York : Artisan, a division of Workman Publishing Co., Inc., [2022]
Identifiers: LCCN 2021048140 | ISBN 9781648291418 (hardback)
Subjects: LCSH: Zodiac.
Classification: LCC BF1726 .S26 2022 | DDC 133.5/2—dc23/eng/20211001
LC record available at https://lccn.loc.gov/2021048140

Book and cover design and illustration by Carlota Santos

Artisan books are available at special discounts when purchased in bulk for premiums and sales promotions as well as for fund-raising or educational use. Special editions or book excerpts also can be created to specification. For details, contact the Special Sales Director at the address below, or send an e-mail to specialmarkets@workman.com.

For speaking engagements, contact speakersbureau@workman.com.

Published by Artisan
A division of Workman Publishing Co., Inc.
225 Varick Street
New York, NY 10014-4381
artisanbooks.com

Artisan is a registered trademark of Workman Publishing Co., Inc.

Printed in China on responsibly sourced paper

First printing, April 2022

1 3 5 7 9 10 8 6 4 2

To my grandfather,
who always asked me
when I was little why
I didn't make a book
with my drawings.

What to Expect from Signs of the Zodiac

Signs of the Zodiac is both an introduction to astrology and a reference book for when you have specific questions. You will learn what a birth chart is and how to interpret it, plus so much more. Let's get started.

Contents

1. Basic Information

Before we dig in, you should familiarize yourself with some definitions:

Astrology: The study of the stars from a mystical, philosophical, and inherently magical point of view. It connects the celestial bodies with how we feel, relate, and manifest; how we evolve; and how cosmic energies influence human life, history, and our relationship with nature.

Astronomy: The study of the celestial bodies of the universe from a scientific and physical perspective. It's important to understand that astronomical decisions and discoveries do not necessarily influence astrology. For example, the constellation Ophiuchus, first written about in the second century CE, is *not* a Zodiac sign (despite the rumor circulating that NASA made it one). The discovery of Uranus, Neptune, and Pluto is a different story, however, as they did become part of astrology, and with them the modern concept of ruling planets emerged.

Constellation: A grouping of stars that form an abstract representation of a mythological character, animal, or object. All cultures have observed, named, and related the constellations to their own mythology.

Horoscope: Part of the most simplified astrology that explains the general characteristics of people born at a certain time. There are many different types of horoscopes (Egyptian, Mayan, and Celtic, for example), yet the most popular one is the Western horoscope, of Greek origin.

Zodiac: The celestial sphere that encompasses the twelve constellations that make up the signs; they are located in the belt through which the ecliptic passes.

Sidereal Zodiac: The eldest Zodiac system, it establishes that the constellations are immobile, static. Due to the movement of the stars, it had to be adjusted periodically, as some constellations are larger than others.

Tropical Zodiac: The Zodiac system that equates the 0 degree of Aries with the beginning of the astral year. By dividing the representation of the celestial sphere mathematically into twelve parts, adjustments are unnecessary. It's the system that we will use as our foundation.

2. MAP OF THE STARS: THE CONSTELLATIONS

The following is the flat representation of the celestial sphere in both hemispheres. It shows the main constellations and how the constellations that represent each Zodiac sign are distributed. You can also see the division of each sign's portion into 30 degrees, as if the map were a clock. This drawing is based on star maps made in the seventeenth and eighteenth centuries that not only were artistic works in themselves but were used to find navigational bearings based on the position of the stars. From our perspective on Earth, it looks like the planets travel from one portion of one Zodiac sign to the next, and that's why people say, "Venus has entered Pisces" or "Mars is in Taurus." "I have Mercury in Pisces," for example, basically means that Mercury was in the Pisces portion when you were born.

Ptolemaic hypothesis
The Earth is presumed to be in the center.

Copernican hypothesis
The Sun is presumed to be in the center and the planets revolve around it; the Moon revolves around the Earth.

The signs of the Zodiac are located on a belt of the sphere centered on the ecliptic. Aries is positioned at the intersection of this belt and the equator (see the figure in the upper right corner on page 13): that's why it is the first sign.

Southern Hemisphere Star Map

HORIZON

Pisces
Cetus
Aries
Phoenix
Lepus
Orion
Corona
Pavo
Southern
Ecliptic Pole
Antarctic
Pole
Chamaeleon
Sirius
Gemini
Antarctic Circle
Lupus
Argo Navis
Centaurus
Tropic of Capricorn
Hydra
Crater

The Ophiuchus
constellation is located
between Scorpio and
Sagittarius, but it's not a
Zodiac sign. A few years back, a
rumor circulated that NASA had
incorporated it into the signs
of the Zodiac. They cannot
make changes to astrology
(see page 10).

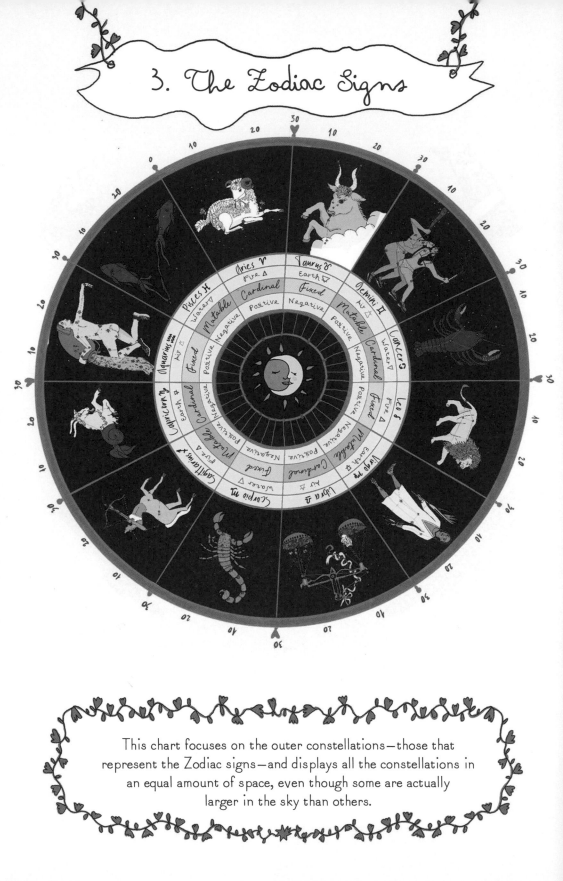

This chart focuses on the outer constellations—those that represent the Zodiac signs—and displays all the constellations in an equal amount of space, even though some are actually larger in the sky than others.

CLASSIFICATION OF THE ZODIAC SIGNS

Below you'll find an overview of each sign's attributes; in the next chapter (page 103), we'll see how the attributes affect each planet.

ELEMENTS (fire, earth, air, water)

FIRE (Aries, Leo, Sagittarius)
Fire signs are dominant, powerful, determined, passionate, impulsive, irascible, tenacious, and charismatic. They have a leadership spirit and are also sociable and enthusiastic. At their worst, they can be aggressive, vain, arrogant, and irritable.

EARTH (Taurus, Virgo, Capricorn)
The earth signs are those who stay on the safe, concrete, and material side. They are creative in a practical way; they need facts, not words, to believe in something. At their worst, they can be stubborn, selfish, and critical.

AIR (Gemini, Libra, Aquarius)
Air signs are dynamic, intellectual, objective, and creative. They love freedom and are sociable and friendly. At their worst, they can be superficial, cold, rebellious, deceitful, and indecisive.

WATER (Cancer, Scorpio, Pisces)
Water signs are emotional, sentimental, and empathetic. With their intuitiveness, they can see beyond the material or superfluous and tend to be interested in the spiritual or mystical. At their worst, they can be infantile, unstable, and scattered.

POLARITIES (positive and negative)

The polarities point to each group of signs' energy in the planet where they are located.

Positive/active/masculine (referred to by all three names)
These are the fire and air signs. Positions in these signs will push the person into action.

Negative/passive/feminine (referred to by all three names)
These are the earth and water signs. Positions in these signs will lead the person to be more traditional and static.

The qualities point to the type of attitude
a person adopts when circumstances change.
The qualities help us clarify a birth chart's
characteristics. Two people can be of the same
element and manifest its nature in completely
different ways depending on their qualities. The
qualities of the signs show if a person is active
and pursues their objectives, or if it's difficult
for them to face change.

CARDINAL SIGNS
(Aries, Cancer, Libra, and Capricorn)

These signs mark the beginning of the seasons: equinox and solstice.
They adopt leadership positions and usually take initiative when
faced with a problem or challenge, especially Aries and Capricorn.
They can be enterprising and exhibit strong willpower.

FIXED SIGNS
(Taurus, Leo, Scorpio, and Aquarius)

These are found in the middle of the seasons (spring, summer, fall, and
winter). They have a more rigid personality than cardinals, so they
prefer rules and structure. They are tough, stubborn, and persevering.
It's difficult for them to handle change.

MUTABLE SIGNS
(Gemini, Virgo, Sagittarius, and Pisces)

These signs denote the end of each season. They have a great ability to
adapt to change and can be unpredictable. They're also versatile,
spontaneous, multiskilled, and contradictory, and they have a tendency
to be irresponsible.

Each sign is associated with a part of the body.

In the Middle Ages, astrology and medicine were closely related. Depending on each person's birth chart, one person was thought to be more prone to suffering from certain ailments than others.

Taurus
Throat, neck, and vertebrae

Cancer
Respiratory system, chest, and lungs

Scorpio
Genitals; infertility problems

Sagittarius
Musculoskeletal system and thighs

Pisces
Feet and nervous system

Aries
Head, skull, and face

Gemini
Upper extremities: arms and shoulders

Leo
Stomach and kidneys

Virgo
Abdomen and intestines

Libra
Buttocks and blood

Capricorn
Skeleton, teeth, and nails

Aquarius
Calves

Beginning on page 19, we will explore each sign individually: its characteristics, the mythological origin of each sign's constellation, and its compatibilities and associations. But remember, to know how compatible two people are, you can't just rely on their Sun sign. You'll have to check the positions of the Sun, Moon, Venus, and Mars in their chart—but we'll get into that later. Right now, on to complementary signs.

THE AXES: COMPLEMENTARY SIGNS

The axes are made up of opposing sign pairs. With different sensitivities, they complement each other perfectly and create strong relationships. In the birth chart of twins, one has the birth sign's energy; the other has the opposite sign's energy, complementary to their sibling—and not just in their Sun sign but also in the other planets (see page 103).

ARIES-LIBRA AXIS

Both signs seek fulfillment. Together, they will reach their goals, as one brings the drive and a certain selfishness (Aries) and the other the balance and harmony (Libra).

TAURUS-SCORPIO AXIS

The passionate and provocative Scorpio finds its opposite in the calm and structured Taurus. They are both feminine, have a fixed quality, are reserved, and don't give up in the face of adversity.

GEMINI-SAGITTARIUS AXIS

These two masculine and mutable signs are open and outgoing, and they adapt well to change. They're also both dynamic, but Sagittarius can have a more philosophical side than Gemini. Gemini provides the fun and teaches Sagittarius not to take life so seriously, and Sagittarius expands Gemini's horizons.

CANCER-CAPRICORN AXIS

They are both feminine and cardinal. Capricorn archetypally contributes everything related to work, structure, and reason, while Cancer is associated with the home, the maternal, and the emotions. Both are conventional and seek security in their partner—Capricorn's realism gives Cancer a sense of security, and Cancer's affection makes Capricorn feel valued.

LEO-AQUARIUS AXIS

Both signs are masculine and fixed signs, outgoing and cheerful. Leo is individualistic, while Aquarius (as an air sign) has values that are more focused on the collective, even on the humanitarian. They are both idealists, they stand out without intending to, and together they can make big changes.

VIRGO-PISCES AXIS

They are mutable and feminine. Virgo is practical and hardworking, while Pisces is dreamy and emotional. They have their vocation to serve others and their compassion in common. Virgo will help ground Pisces, and Pisces will help Virgo look far beyond the material and rational.

Aries

MARCH 21 – APRIL 20

RULING PLANET: Mars

ELEMENT: Fire

QUALITY: Cardinal
POLARITY: Positive/
masculine

FIRST HOUSE:
Individuality,
self-image

Whether your Sun is in Aries or you have another planet in this sign, the most distinctive Aries trait is being energetic and enthusiastic. Aries individuals can be somewhat argumentative, even stubborn and aggressive (although they will deny it). Since they're the first Zodiac sign, it's easy to remember what role they usually take: leader. Aries are very clear about when, how, and why they do things, and they enjoy giving instructions so that everything goes perfectly. Of course, problems may arise when it comes time to negotiate, especially with people slower or quieter than them—Aries can become quite impatient. They can also be somewhat jealous or possessive, but are ultimately a charismatic sign with a dazzling self-confidence.

ARIES
Fire sign, cardinal and masculine
March 21-April 20

VIRTUES: They are natural leaders, self-assured, optimistic, direct, energetic, and active. They have a lot of drive. They're generous and not duplicitous. Their anger passes quickly. They are daring, know how to defend themselves, and are brave, sociable, and flirtatious.

FLAWS: They are hot-tempered and impulsive. They lack self-control. They can be bossy. They don't like taking orders. They're so direct that they can be insensitive. They have a tendency to whine. They risk too much, are self-centered and materialistic, and have little patience.

FAMOUS ARIES: Quentin Tarantino, Mariah Carey, Robert Downey Jr., and Lady Gaga

Constellation

The Aries constellation is located between the Pisces constellation (to the west) and the Taurus constellation (to the east). Other nearby constellations are Perseus, the Triangle, and Cetus (see the star maps on pages 12-13).

Arietis is its brightest star, followed by Sheratan, Mesarthim, and Botein. Its name comes from Sanskrit, the language of India and one of the oldest in the world, and from Arabic. Arietis is also known as Hamal, the "ram's head" in Arabic.

Aries's Ruling Planet: Mars

As you will see in "The Astrological Planets" (page 103), Mars is Aries's ruling planet. He is the Roman god of war. He is also related to active sexual energy, violence, and impulsiveness. All these characteristics are reflected to a greater or lesser extent in this passionate and active sign.

Aries has Venus in detriment, the Sun in exaltation, and Saturn in fall. This will be explained in the next chapter (page 103).

How to Manage Aries Energy

Whether you have the Sun or other planets in Aries (see "The Astrological Planets," page 103), certain characteristics may apply to you. Let's explore how to make the most of this intense and passionate energy.

Generally, Aries should strive to be more patient and tolerant with others, and to develop consistency. They have a lot of energy, so it would be beneficial for them to practice some sport or physical activity to reduce aggressiveness and focus all that vigor on something positive. They may tend to be somewhat dominant with their partner, which is not necessarily a negative thing, but they should be careful not to hurt other people's feelings. If you are an Aries and you do not identify with this description, remember that you'll need to calculate your birth chart (see page 152) to see what other types of energy you have and what characteristics you carry from other signs. If Mars were in this sign, it would be powerful, and the person would be very sexual and possibly impulsive and risky in their love life, as you will see later.

Amulets for Aries

Aries is an energetic and determined sign. The best amulets to help them take advantage of all that energy are those that help them relax and make decisions with less impulsiveness, as well as amulets that enhance positive qualities.

Name	Type of Amulet		Purpose
Ruby	Red gemstone		Balances their possessive side. Helps enhance their mood and balance their energy.
Amethyst	Lavender or red gemstone		Balances and calms; aids in avoiding frustration and anger.
Red jasper	Red (semiprecious) stone		Protects from negative energies; increases patience and will.
Diamond	Transparent gemstone		Aries's lucky stone. Enhances their natural brightness and symbolizes power.
Tulip	Flower		Friendship flower. Enhances enthusiasm and energy. Red tulips are ideal.
Red	Color		Aries's lucky color. If you are an Aries and you feel down, try wearing a red ribbon or garment; it's the color of your ruling planet, Mars.

Corresponding Tarot Card: The Emperor

Each sign has a corresponding tarot card that symbolizes some of its characteristics. In the case of Aries, it's the Emperor. It represents power, strength, a brilliant person with authority; however, its negative side can be related to violence and abuse of power.

Ritual for Aries to Enhance Perseverance and Attract Good Vibes

You'll need:

3 yellow candles
1 amethyst
1 white cloth
Matches

METHOD:
The night before your birthday, form a triangle with the candles and place the amethyst in the center. Light the candles, think of all the goals you want to accomplish, and leave the candles lit until they burn out. On your birthday, wrap the amethyst in a white cloth, then carry it with you for ten days.

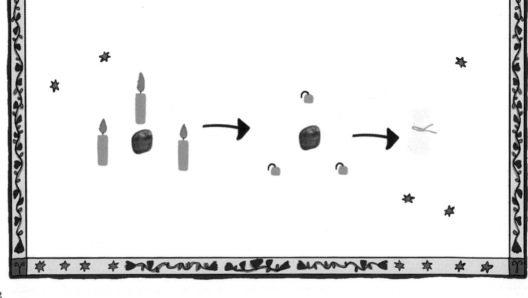

Aries Compatibilities

Remember to check your Moon, Venus, and
Mars signs in addition to the Sun sign.

+ (ANOTHER) ARIES
♡ ♡ ♡ ♡ ♡ ♡ ♡ ♡ ♡ ♡

Both of their strong
characters and irascibility
can cause conflicts, but on a
sexual and mental level they
are compatible.

+ TAURUS
♡ ♡ ♡ ♡ ♡ ♡ ♡ ♡ ♡ ♡

Aries is impatient, and
Taurus may find Aries
too aggressive. Both are
stubborn and uncompromising,
but their shared appreciation
for the pleasures of life may
bring them closer together.

+ GEMINI
♡ ♡ ♡ ♡ ♡ ♡ ♡ ♡ ♡ ♡

There is a strong attraction
between these two. Aries
finds Gemini's eloquence
fascinating, and Gemini
admires Aries's confidence.
They can tire of each other,
given that both are
unpredictable.

+ CANCER
♡ ♡ ♡ ♡ ♡ ♡ ♡ ♡ ♡ ♡

Cancer is very sensitive,
and the abruptness of Aries
can cause the relationship to
not prosper. Both will have
to make a concerted effort to
understand each other.

+ LEO
♡ ♡ ♡ ♡ ♡ ♡ ♡ ♡ ♡ ♡

Very good couple, one of the
best in the Zodiac. They will
protect and motivate each
other—together they are
invincible.

+ VIRGO
♡ ♡ ♡ ♡ ♡ ♡ ♡ ♡ ♡ ♡

Virgo's analytical mind
has nothing to do with the
dynamic and impulsive Aries
mind. It will take serious
effort on both sides to
understand each other.

+ LIBRA
♡ ♡ ♡ ♡ ♡ ♡ ♡ ♡ ♡ ♡

Libra will bring balance
to Aries and this will give
Libra determination. Both
are somewhat materialistic;
they should be wary of
codependency.

+ SCORPIO
♡ ♡ ♡ ♡ ♡ ♡ ♡ ♡ ♡ ♡

Both signs are intense:
physically, they are
compatible, but emotionally,
Scorpio can find Aries
impulsive and superficial,
and Aries may think Scorpio
is a little strange and
pessimistic.

+ SAGITTARIUS
♡ ♡ ♡ ♡ ♡ ♡ ♡ ♡ ♡ ♡

Although Sagittarius is
somewhat more carefree and
independent, their energies
are in sync. They are both
passionate, dynamic, and
fun-loving.

+ CAPRICORN
♡ ♡ ♡ ♡ ♡ ♡ ♡ ♡ ♡ ♡

The coldness of Capricorn
collides head-on with the
passionate disposition
of Aries. It's a type of
complication that can work,
but it will take a lot of effort.

+ AQUARIUS
♡ ♡ ♡ ♡ ♡ ♡ ♡ ♡ ♡ ♡

They have fun together, but
Aries's jealousy can take
a toll, and Aquarius's desire
for freedom can make Aries
feel insecure. Although
there is attraction, it can
get complicated.

+ PISCES
♡ ♡ ♡ ♡ ♡ ♡ ♡ ♡ ♡ ♡

Although attraction may
exist, Aries will tend to
dominate Pisces. Pisces can
become complacent and lose
themselves in Aries's strong
character.

THE MYTH THAT GIVES RISE TO ARIES:

The Golden Fleece

The constellation Aries represents a ram, specifically that of the Greek myth of the Golden Fleece. Although the ram appears in several stories, the most important include the one that describes the origin of the constellation and the story of Jason and the Argonauts.

Following is the first one:

King Athamas had two children, Helle and Phrixus, from his first marriage to Queen Nephele. When she passed away, he married Ino. She was cruel and planned to murder her husband's two children so that her children would inherit the kingdom. But the god Hermes (or Zeus, depending on the version), who was watching it all unfold, took pity on Helle and Phrixus and sent them a magical winged ram (the fleece) to save them. The animal flew them to new lands, but as they escaped, Helle fell into the sea and died. After the mishap, Phrixus no longer trusted the fleece's flying skills and continued his journey with it on foot. He walked until he reached the sacred forest of Ares, which belonged to King Aeëtes. The king welcomed Phrixus and, in gratitude (or because he was fed up with the fleece), Phrixus sacrificed the ram and left it hanging from an oak tree in the forest.

The gods, seeing that the fleece had done its job (ignoring the fact that one of the siblings died), turned it into a constellation so that it would always be remembered.

The second story begins later, when Jason, the son of Aeson, was born. Jason was the rightful heir to the throne of Iolcus, but his father's brother, Pelias, had taken over. The Oracle warned Pelias, "You have usurped the throne; know that one of your brother's descendants will seek revenge." Pelias knew that the Oracle was talking about Jason, so he ordered him to undertake an almost impossible task: to recover the Golden Fleece. And so Jason began his journey: the Argonautic. The story of Jason and the Argonauts is one of the most well known in mythology.

For the mission to be successful, Jason recruited the best warriors, the greatest heroes of Greece, including Hercules and Orpheus. After a long and eventful journey, they reached Colchis, where Jason asked King Aeëtes to give him the Golden Fleece. The king consented but on the condition that Jason pass a difficult test: plowing the land using two bulls with metal legs that spewed flames from their nostrils, then sowing some dragon's teeth. Aeëtes did not warn Jason that by sowing those teeth, an army would come out of the earth to attack him.

Medea, the daughter of Aeëtes, fell in love with Jason. She gave him an ointment that would make him invincible and told him about her father's plan. Jason passed the test, killed the dragon guarding the fleece, and escaped with Medea. They returned to Pelias's kingdom after much trouble, and the story had a happy ending.

ARIES-TAURUS CUSP

April 19-April 25

Cusps are people born in the days immediately before and after the astrological seasonal change. People born on those dates may identify with traits of both the earlier and later signs. Depending on the rest of their birth chart, they may feel akin to their Sun sign or to the other sign close to their birth date.

The Aries–Taurus summit is characterized by giving its natives two of the best characteristics of both signs: Aries's drive and Taurus's tenacity. They will have leading ideas in their field, initiative, and entrepreneurship, and the perseverance necessary to not lose enthusiasm over time.

Aries's energetic character finds stability with the undertones of Taurus. But the flammable character of Aries also joins the stubbornness of Taurus, which can lead to stubborn and short-tempered people who are also loyal and protective.

Taurus
APRIL 21 – MAY 20

RULING PLANET: Venus

ELEMENT: Earth

QUALITY: Fixed
POLARITY:
Negative/feminine

SECOND HOUSE:
Materialistic,
intellectual,
talented, skillful

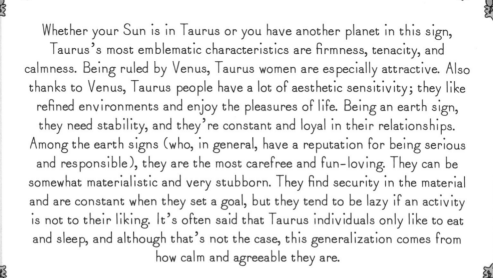

Whether your Sun is in Taurus or you have another planet in this sign, Taurus's most emblematic characteristics are firmness, tenacity, and calmness. Being ruled by Venus, Taurus women are especially attractive. Also thanks to Venus, Taurus people have a lot of aesthetic sensitivity; they like refined environments and enjoy the pleasures of life. Being an earth sign, they need stability, and they're constant and loyal in their relationships. Among the earth signs (who, in general, have a reputation for being serious and responsible), they are the most carefree and fun-loving. They can be somewhat materialistic and very stubborn. They find security in the material and are constant when they set a goal, but they tend to be lazy if an activity is not to their liking. It's often said that Taurus individuals only like to eat and sleep, and although that's not the case, this generalization comes from how calm and agreeable they are.

TAURUS
Earth sign, fixed and feminine
April 21-May 20

VIRTUES: They are patient, friendly, serene, reliable, constant, faithful, and loyal. When it comes to making decisions, they're level-headed. They're also realistic, sensible, practical, domestic, and prudent.

FLAWS: They are intolerant, obstinate, and proud; they are slow in making decisions, stubborn, passive, and materialistic, and have little initiative. They're sedentary and pigheaded.

FAMOUS TAURUSES: Jessica Alba, Megan Fox, Travis Scott, Gigi Hadid, Robert Pattinson, Cher, Penélope Cruz, and Queen Elizabeth II of England

Constellation

The brightest star in the constellation Taurus is Aldebaran. Although it had been observed in ancient times, its name is Arabic and means "the one that follows," since it seems to follow the Pleiades cluster. Aldebaran is very close to the ecliptic, and the Moon covers it frequently and at regular intervals. Beta Tauri and Zeta Tauri are the stars that form the bull's horns.

Taurus's Ruling Planet: Venus

As you will see in "The Astrological Planets" (page 103), Venus is the Roman goddess of love and beauty. She's connected to aesthetics and romantic attraction. Being a feminine sign ruled by Venus, Taurus women are usually sensual and attractive and have luxurious taste.

Fields such as design, decoration, or fashion are areas in which Taurus can excel, as well as anything to do with caring for the unprotected, such as nursing or medicine. Additionally, Taurus people tend to be animal lovers, and they like children.

In Greek culture, the goddess equivalent to Venus is Aphrodite, from whom the word *aphrodisiac* comes, meaning "it gives pleasure and enjoyment."

Taurus has Mars in detriment, the Moon in exaltation, and Uranus in fall. This will be explained in the next chapter (page 103).

How to Manage Taurus Energy

Whether you have the Sun or other planets in Taurus (see "The Astrological Planets," page 103), certain characteristics may apply to you. Let's see how to make the most of this constant and calm energy.

In general, over the course of their lives, Taurus people must learn to be more tolerant of others, less stubborn, and less proud. This does not mean they have to change the way they are, but they must learn to be more flexible to reach their full potential.

A good exercise for Taurus is to houseclean and get rid of things they don't use. Taurus tends to accumulate possessions, and it's good to discard items that no longer satisfy to find better or more rewarding ones. When Taurus gets organized and decides what things to throw away, they can acknowledge the role those objects played in their life, then let them go.

Amulets for Taurus

Taurus is a calm and carefree sign. The best amulets for this sign are those that attract security and material goods, in addition to amulets that help them let go of situations, people, or objects that no longer bring them happiness.

Name	Type of Amulet		Purpose
Lapis lazuli	Blue (semiprecious) stone		Helps to deepen Taurus's spirituality and find their destiny and divine purpose.
Blue tourmaline	Blue (semiprecious) stone		Enhances intuition and quick decision-making, as well as spirituality.
Emerald	Green gemstone		Strengthens love, understanding, empathy, and tolerance.
Pink quartz	Pink (semiprecious) stone		Stone associated with Venus, the goddess of love and ruling planet of Taurus; reinforces compassion.
Daisy	Flower		Harmony flower. Builds resilience and kindness.
Pink	Color		Taurus's lucky color. If they feel sad or misunderstood, they should wear a pink garment or accessory. It brings harmony, sweetness, and balance.

Corresponding Tarot Card: The High Priest

Each sign has a corresponding tarot card that symbolizes some of its characteristics. In the case of Taurus, it's the High Priest. Taurus relates to tradition, objectiveness, calmness, and the well established, just like this card.

Ritual for Taurus to Attract Money and Prosperity

You'll need:

1 silver chain
1 white candle
1 green candle
1 white rose

METHOD:
The night before your birthday, form a circle with the chain. Place the rose in the circle and flank it with the candles. Light the candles and say: "Lady of Luck, bless me with your light, attract for me money and fortune. Lady of Luck, enlighten me with your light." Wait for the candles to burn out.

Taurus Compatibilities

Remember to check your Moon, Venus, and Mars signs in addition to the Sun sign.

+ (ANOTHER) TAURUS
♥ ♥ ♥ ♥ ♥ ♥ ♥ ♥ ♡ ♡

Taurus partners are calm and constant. Their inflexibility might lead to rubbing each other the wrong way. They're stubborn and they could possibly get stuck in a routine (although they love the predictability).

+ GEMINI
♥ ♥ ♥ ♡ ♡ ♡ ♡ ♡ ♡ ♡

Gemini's independence, quick thinking, and changeable mind can confuse traditional, laid-back Taurus. It will take effort on both sides to make this work, and a lot of tact.

+ CANCER
♥ ♥ ♥ ♥ ♡ ♥ ♡ ♡ ♡ ♡

Although Cancer's temperament is somewhat unpredictable, Taurus's patience can handle these mood swings. Taurus knows that under the crab's surface lies a loving person who enjoys life to its fullest, just like the bull.

+ LEO
♥ ♥ ♡ ♡ ♡ ♡ ♡ ♡ ♡ ♡

Leo's charisma may fascinate Taurus at first, and Leo will enjoy Taurus's attention. However, Leo loves to fool around and is quite selfish, which Taurus may not understand. If both parties put in the work, it can be a positive relationship.

+ VIRGO
♥ ♥ ♥ ♥ ♡ ♥ ♥ ♥ ♥ ♡

Since they are both earth signs, they will be laid-back. Virgo will be somewhat more cerebral than Taurus, who prefers to enjoy life and relax. Virgo can help Taurus be more active, and Taurus can help Virgo let loose.

+ LIBRA
♥ ♥ ♥ ♥ ♡ ♡ ♡ ♡ ♡ ♡

Both ruled by Venus, they will find inspiration, harmony, and beauty in each other. But Libra is more volatile than Taurus, and Taurus may feel that their emotional needs are being neglected.

+ SCORPIO
♥ ♥ ♥ ♥ ♡ ♥ ♥ ♡ ♡ ♡

Taurus can find the security they seek in this loyal and emotionally intense sign. Scorpio may be more mysterious and sensitive than Taurus, but passion and lasting love are possible.

+ SAGITTARIUS
♥ ♡ ♡ ♡ ♡ ♡ ♡ ♡ ♡ ♡

Sagittarius cannot stand still: this will lead to a head-on collision with thoughtful and leisurely Taurus. For the relationship to work, both will have to respect each other's space and time.

+ CAPRICORN
♥ ♥ ♥ ♥ ♥ ♥ ♥ ♥ ♥ ♡

Although Capricorn is more ambitious, both have traditional values and need security. Capricorn's drive and Taurus's steadfastness will make this a great match.

+ AQUARIUS
♥ ♥ ♡ ♡ ♡ ♡ ♡ ♡ ♡ ♡

Although Taurus's confidence may seem intriguing to Aquarius, their emotional needs are very different. Aquarius is independent and changeable, and Taurus tends to put their peace before the comings and goings of Aquarius.

+ PISCES
♥ ♥ ♥ ♥ ♡ ♥ ♥ ♡ ♡ ♡

The sensitivity of Pisces and the constancy of Taurus can complement each other well. The problem may be Pisces's emotional changes, as Taurus is more constant and inflexible. Pisces's tenderness can be irresistible to Taurus.

+ ARIES
♥ ♥ ♡ ♡ ♡ ♡ ♡ ♡ ♡ ♡

Both are so stubborn and uncompromising that getting along will be difficult. Aries's impulsiveness may seem incomprehensible to Taurus, and Aries may view the bull as slow and lacking spark.

The Abduction of Europa

It's no secret that Zeus is the biggest Olympian playboy god ever. When he liked a mortal, he had no problem kidnapping her, raping her, and simply moving on. The myth of Europa is one of those Zeus infatuation stories. In this case, the girl in question was, of course, very beautiful and enjoyed doing normal girlish things, like picking flowers in fields. Europa was walking with her friends in one of these fields when she met Zeus, who had turned himself into a white bull. Seeing the animal (and not knowing it was actually a lustful god), Europa approached and caressed him, fascinated by his beauty. She made him a garland of flowers, and when she realized he was tame, she climbed on his back. Zeus seized his chance and ran off with Europa to Crete.

To show her his love and to demonstrate that he had no bad intentions, Zeus formed a constellation that re-created the white bull, the shape that he had chosen to deceive and kidnap Europa. To Zeus it must have seemed like the height of romanticism. This is the origin of the constellation Taurus, which is located between the constellations Aries and Gemini.

Europa was welcomed by the king of Crete, who later married her and adopted her three children by Zeus. The earliest mention of this myth is in the *Iliad* and in Hesiod's *Catalog of Women*. A more benign version tells how Zeus kidnaps Europa but reveals his true identity when they arrive in Crete, and she consents to his desires.

It's said that Zeus gave Europa additional gifts to commemorate their meeting: a necklace made by Hephaestus (the blacksmith god); Talos, a bronze automaton; Laelaps, a dog that never let go of its prey; and a spear that never missed its mark.

The abduction of Europa has been an inspiration for many artists: Titian, Rubens, Rembrandt, and Picasso.

The Cretan Bull

There are other myths around the bull. One such is that of the Minotaur and the Cretan Bull, described in the Twelve Labors of Heracles. In this story, Minos, the king of Crete, promised to make an offering to Poseidon, the god of the sea. So Poseidon sent a great, handsome bull out of the sea, but when Minos saw the bull, he was so impressed that instead of sacrificing it to Poseidon as agreed, he decided to keep it. Obviously, Poseidon found that an unforgivable lack of respect and planned his revenge: he made Minos's wife, Pasiphae, fall in love with the bull. Months later, the queen gave birth to a strange creature, half man and half bull: the Minotaur. King Minos was very affected and had the Minotaur locked up. (What happened to the Minotaur is another story.)

As for Poseidon's famous bull, he was strong and untamable in addition to big and beautiful. It was Heracles who ultimately handled him and took him out of Crete. Heracles tried to offer the bull to the gods as an offering, but no one wanted it. No longer knowing what to do with the animal, Heracles set him free. The bull wreaked havoc in various towns and cities until the hero Theseus ended the animal's life once and for all.

Taurus Season

May 17

May 23

Gemini Season

TAURUS-GEMINI CUSP

May 17- May 23

Cusps are people born in the days immediately before and after the astrological seasonal change. People born on those dates may identify with traits of both the earlier and later signs. Depending on the rest of their birth chart, they may feel akin to their Sun sign or to the other sign close to their birth date.

The Taurus–Gemini summit is characterized by giving its natives two of the best traits of both signs: the constancy of Taurus and the curiosity of Gemini. These people seem serious, stable, and trustworthy like a Taurus, but they're full of surprises. They have the sense of innovation and quirky ideas characteristic of air signs.

They can confuse their partner, since on the one hand they demand a lot of trust but on the other they need their space and plenty of freedom and independence.

Gemini

MAY 21 – JUNE 20

RULING PLANET: Mercury

ELEMENT: Air

QUALITY: Mutable
POLARITY: Positive/
masculine

THIRD HOUSE:
Communication,
childhood,
family

Whether your Sun is in Gemini or you have another planet in this sign, Gemini's most distinctive characteristics are ease of communication, adaptability, and creativity. Gemini people have a great ability to find innovative solutions and convey them in an appealing way; they are sociable, open, and always ready to learn new things. It's a dual sign; in other words, on the one hand they have this more outgoing side, but on the other they're profound people who need independence and solitude. Among the air signs, which are generally outgoing, Gemini could be said to be the most intellectual. They can be good writers, speakers, or comedians; have a great sense of humor; and enjoy talking. They're very independent, and their ideal partner is someone who respects their space and doesn't clip their wings, entices them with new topics, and isn't scandalized by their wild ideas.

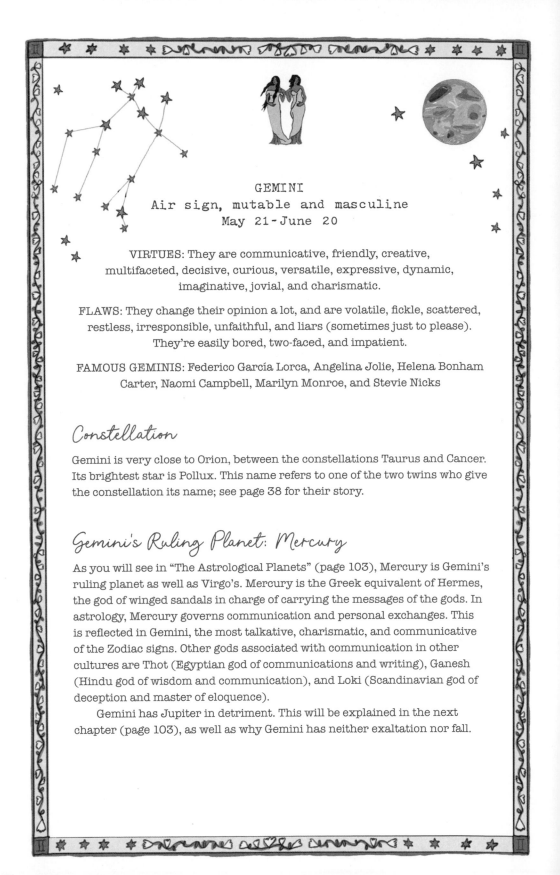

GEMINI
Air sign, mutable and masculine
May 21–June 20

VIRTUES: They are communicative, friendly, creative, multifaceted, decisive, curious, versatile, expressive, dynamic, imaginative, jovial, and charismatic.

FLAWS: They change their opinion a lot, and are volatile, fickle, scattered, restless, irresponsible, unfaithful, and liars (sometimes just to please). They're easily bored, two-faced, and impatient.

FAMOUS GEMINIS: Federico García Lorca, Angelina Jolie, Helena Bonham Carter, Naomi Campbell, Marilyn Monroe, and Stevie Nicks

Constellation

Gemini is very close to Orion, between the constellations Taurus and Cancer. Its brightest star is Pollux. This name refers to one of the two twins who give the constellation its name; see page 38 for their story.

Gemini's Ruling Planet: Mercury

As you will see in "The Astrological Planets" (page 103), Mercury is Gemini's ruling planet as well as Virgo's. Mercury is the Greek equivalent of Hermes, the god of winged sandals in charge of carrying the messages of the gods. In astrology, Mercury governs communication and personal exchanges. This is reflected in Gemini, the most talkative, charismatic, and communicative of the Zodiac signs. Other gods associated with communication in other cultures are Thot (Egyptian god of communications and writing), Ganesh (Hindu god of wisdom and communication), and Loki (Scandinavian god of deception and master of eloquence).

Gemini has Jupiter in detriment. This will be explained in the next chapter (page 103), as well as why Gemini has neither exaltation nor fall.

How to Manage Gemini Energy

Whether you have the Sun or other planets in Gemini (see "The Astrological Planets," page 103), certain characteristics may apply to you. Let's see how to make the most of this sign's dispersed and open energy.

Generally, Geminis will have to learn to be more constant to make the most of their creativity. They will be good communicators and very charismatic, but they need to develop empathy and a certain strategy. In relationships, if they do not have positions in water or land that contradict these traits, they will have a fear of commitment and will often get bored if their partner doesn't provide new stimuli and fun situations. If you are a Gemini and don't identify with this description, remember that by calculating your birth chart (see page 152), you'll be able to see what other types of energy you have and what characteristics you carry from other signs. A calm and stable Moon, for instance, such as the Moon in Taurus, would nullify a fear of commitment and make this person seek and stay in more stable relationships. A very powerful position for Gemini is Mercury; individuals born in this position will have great speaking skills and creativity.

Amulets for Gemini

Gemini people are scattered and creative. The best amulets, for this reason, are those that reinforce their creativity but also help them concentrate and have greater perseverance and patience.

Name	Type of Amulet		Purpose
Opal	Blue (semiprecious) stone		"Dual" jewel, representing the duality of this sign. Helps to unite Gemini's dual nature and calms them.
Topaz	Yellow (semiprecious) stone		Awakens creativity, balances emotions, and brings good luck.
Beryllium	Green (semiprecious) stone		Associated with intelligence. Ideal for meditation and relaxation when making decisions.
Aquamarine	Greenish blue (semiprecious) stone		Gemini's lucky stone. Enhances their charm and reasoning.
Rose	Flower		Like Gemini, it has a dual nature: thorns and beauty.
Yellow	Color		Gemini's lucky color. Related to intellect, reason, and concentration. Helps realize Gemini's creative projects.

Corresponding Tarot Card: The Lovers

Each sign has a corresponding tarot card that symbolizes some of its characteristics. In Gemini's case, it's the Lovers. The card symbolizes not only couple relationships but also personal or business exchanges.

Ritual for Gemini to Encourage Perseverance

You'll need:

Graphite pencil
Paper

METHOD:
Tapping into this sign's communication skills, on the night before your birthday, write a letter to yourself. Write down your strengths, your goals, and your visions for the future. Keep the paper under your mattress and read it whenever you feel discouraged and are tempted to set aside your goals.

Gemini Compatibilities

Remember to check your Moon, Venus, and
Mars signs in addition to the Sun sign.

+ (ANOTHER) GEMINI
♥ ♥ ♥ ♡ ♡ ♡ ♡ ♡ ♡ ♡

Both will enjoy each other's company, and they'll never get bored. Being somewhat fickle, the two may not materialize a formal relationship, but the laughs are guaranteed.

+ CANCER
♥ ♥ ♥ ♡ ♡ ♡ ♡ ♡ ♡ ♡

Cancer seeks safety, home, and protection. Gemini looks for change, adventure, and innovation in their relationships, so reaching an agreement between these two can be quite complicated.

+ LEO
♥ ♥ ♥ ♥ ♡ ♡ ♡ ♡ ♡ ♡

There is a strong pull between the two signs, but they both tend to be individualistic. Leo may seem somewhat selfish and superficial to Gemini, as well as jealous.

+ VIRGO
♥ ♥ ♥ ♡ ♡ ♡ ♡ ♡ ♡ ♡

The routine, stability, and order of Virgo collide head-on with the dynamism of Gemini. Although they share a ruler, Virgo is more analytical and calmer than Gemini.

+ LIBRA
♥ ♥ ♥ ♥ ♥ ♡ ♡ ♡ ♡ ♡

Although Gemini may find Libra somewhat sensitive and dependent, Libra will go out of their way to please Gemini and respect their space. The two converse fluently and have similar tastes.

+ SCORPIO
♥ ♥ ♥ ♥ ♡ ♡ ♡ ♡ ♡ ♡

Complicated combination. Scorpio's possessiveness can manifest itself, as Gemini doesn't offer this sign the security it needs. Gemini can feel drowned out by Scorpio's intensity.

+ SAGITTARIUS
♥ ♥ ♥ ♥ ♥ ♥ ♥ ♥ ♥ ♡

Great chemistry. They both need freedom. Sagittarius will open up new horizons for Gemini, helping them discover new interests and hobbies. Guaranteed adventures.

+ CAPRICORN
♥ ♥ ♥ ♡ ♡ ♡ ♡ ♡ ♡ ♡

Although there may be attraction at first, Capricorn seeks stability and security that Gemini may find boring. A good combination in friendship.

+ AQUARIUS
♥ ♥ ♥ ♥ ♥ ♥ ♥ ♥ ♡ ♡

Intellectually they'll be compatible, and both will respect each other's time and space. Aquarius has a more humanitarian side, which will expand Gemini's horizons.

+ PISCES
♥ ♥ ♥ ♥ ♥ ♡ ♡ ♡ ♡ ♡

Pisces's sensitivity and daydreaming can make Gemini fly, but they are both inconsistent, and Pisces can be hurt by Gemini's erratic behavior.

+ ARIES
♥ ♥ ♥ ♥ ♥ ♡ ♡ ♡ ♡ ♡

Strong attraction—both enjoy going out, having fun, and socializing. But Aries's jealousy and explosiveness can baffle Gemini and make them feel like a prisoner.

+ TAURUS
♥ ♥ ♥ ♡ ♡ ♡ ♡ ♡ ♡ ♡

Gemini may find Taurus boring and their slowness in making decisions exasperating. Taurus's bullfighting stubbornness and Gemini's continuous change make it difficult for them to get along.

THE MYTH THAT GIVES RISE TO GEMINI:
Castor and Pollux

There are several versions of this myth, and some contradict each other. Let's explore the most widespread one.

Leda was the wife of Tyndareus, king of Sparta. They loved each other very much. Leda was beautiful and Zeus, of course, took a fancy to her. Since he knew that Leda loved her husband and that (even though he was the god of Olympus) she wouldn't want to tryst with him, Zeus came up with an idea, as always of dubious morality: he became a swan and tricked Leda into sleeping with him. She got pregnant by Zeus, but shortly after she did the deed with her husband and also got pregnant by him. So Leda carried a double pregnancy: one from Zeus as a swan and one from her husband.

Nine months later, Leda found out she was expecting two sets of twins and gave birth to a mortal boy and girl (Castor and Clytemnestra) and an egg. The egg hatched, and the other pair of twins were born: Pollux and Helena. Two mortal children of the king, and two semi-divine children of Zeus. Two boys and two girls. The girls take a back seat in this story, so let's focus on Castor and Pollux.

Although Castor and Pollux were children of different parents, they were inseparable, they loved each other dearly, and they were strikingly similar physically. As they grew older, they became skilled warriors.

One day Castor had an accident and died. Pollux, filled with sorrow, begged his father, Zeus, to grant his brother immortality. Zeus, deeply moved, decided to grant immortality to both of them. Thus Zeus created a constellation in honor of these close brothers, and that is the origin of the constellation Gemini.

Gemini Representation

Despite their mythological origin as male twins, the astrological image of Gemini can be depicted by two female figures. This representation came later and was popularized in the horoscopes of the twentieth century; today it's more popular and widespread than that of the legendary Castor and Pollux, who were depicted wearing eggshell-shaped helmets, Castor with a whip (he was a skilled horse trainer) and Pollux with a club (he was an expert in hand-to-hand combat).

The two Gemini women, on the other hand, are usually represented in long dresses and similar hairstyles. The illustration in this chapter can be considered a middle ground: two almost identical female figures in modern outfits, but with weapons in their hands—a version of the whip but with carnations and a club with more flowers, to represent the Gemini duality between their passion for art and their more expansive side.

Gemini Season
June 19
June 23
Cancer Season

June 19-June 23

Cusps are people born in the days immediately before and after the astrological seasonal change. People born on those dates may identify with traits of both the earlier and later signs. Depending on the rest of their birth chart, they may feel akin to their Sun sign or to the other sign close to their birth date.

The Gemini-Cancer summit is characterized by its sensitivity to art and communication from a sublime and poetic point of view. They are good at expressing themselves on a metaphorical level, have a sense of humor, and tend to get carried away by feelings rather than reason. They have a great ability to read emotions. They are intuitive and reasonable, and routines can seem boring to them.

On the downside, they have a short attention span and tend to be a bit lazy.

Cancer

JUNE 21 – JULY 22

RULING PLANET: Moon

ELEMENT: Water

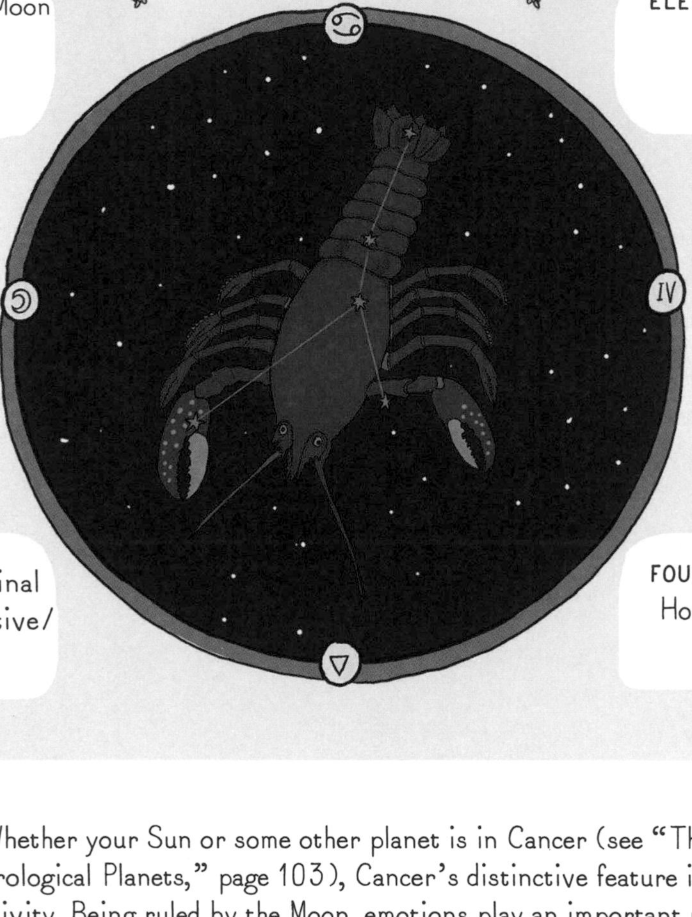

QUALITY: Cardinal
POLARITY: Negative/
feminine

FOURTH HOUSE:
Home, safety,
family

Whether your Sun or some other planet is in Cancer (see "The Astrological Planets," page 103), Cancer's distinctive feature is its sensitivity. Being ruled by the Moon, emotions play an important role in this sign. Cancers are contradictory: sensitive, yet introspective; sweet, yet irritable; materialistic, yet homey. Cancer values are usually traditional: they cherish spending time with family, and despite their extreme sensitivity, they have a strong character that they don't hesitate to display when they or their family feel threatened. Among the water signs, it's the most maternal one. Despite such a rich emotional world, they tend to have frequent mood swings. They seem quite mysterious, since they don't like to show their vulnerable side—that's why their character is the least clear in the Zodiac. Sometimes they're shy, other times they're outgoing and unpredictable . . . with Cancer, you never know.

CANCER
Water sign, cardinal and feminine
June 21-July 22

VIRTUES: They are homey, sensitive, maternal, jovial, imaginative, idealistic, affectionate, thoughtful, romantic, flirtatious, sweet, expressive, and caring.

FLAWS: They are insecure, lazy, spiteful, withdrawn, fanciful, contradictory, wasteful, sentimental, apprehensive, hypochondriacal, cranky, and have volatile mood swings.

FAMOUS CANCERS: Frida Kahlo, Courtney Love, Princess Diana, Selena Gomez, and Ariana Grande

Constellation

The constellation Cancer is the least bright one in the Zodiac. It's surrounded by the constellations Lynx, Gemini, Canis Minor, Hydra, and Leo.

Its most prominent stars are Alpha Cancri or Acubens, Beta Cancri or Tarf, Delta Cancri (a double star that's close to the ecliptic, so it's sometimes hidden by the Moon), Gamma Cancri, Iota Cancri, and Zeta Cancri or Tegmine.

Cancer's Ruling Planet: The Moon

As you will see in "The Astrological Planets" (page 103), the Moon is Cancer's ruling planet. It has been linked in many cultures to emotions, the occult, motherhood, witches, and feminine power. Since Cancers are ruled by the Moon, like the sea they have comings and goings: they rise and fall. Cancer's emotional world is known for being volatile: they go from joy to sadness, from sadness to anger, and from anger to rage or happiness in short intervals. In ancient times, the Moon was related to Selene, daughter of the Titans Hyperion and Theia. Later, Artemis and Selene were considered the same goddess.

Cancer has Saturn in detriment, Jupiter in exaltation, and Mars in fall. This will be explained in the next chapter (page 103).

How to Manage Cancer Energy

Whether you have the Sun or other planets in Cancer (see "The Astrological Planets," page 103), certain characteristics may apply to you. Let's explore how to make the most of this changing and emotional energy.

Typically, over the course of their lives, Cancers will need to learn to balance their emotions. It's not an easy task, but activities such as keeping a journal, meditating, or looking for artistic ways to express their emotions can be of great help. The point is to channel their sensitivity through a healthy means of expression rather than repress or reject this emotional side, which could lead to insecurity and shyness. When well managed, Cancers can be sociable and friendly people.

Amulets for Cancer

The most appropriate amulets for this sign are those that help balance their sensitive side, their emotions, and their mood swings, as well as those that reinforce confidence.

Name	Type of amulet	Purpose
Shells	Marine origin	Shells on the beach connect Cancer with the sea and the Moon, providing them with balance. The shells must not come from slaughtered aquatic species.
Pearl	Marine origin	Connects with the sea, femininity, Aphrodite, the Moon; highlights qualities such as femininity and sensitivity.
Turquoise	Blue-green (semiprecious) stone	Offers luck and protection to Cancer natives.
Moonstone	White (semiprecious) stone	Balances the emotional side, calms the nerves, and drives away worries.
Water lily	Flower	Aquatic flower. A reminder of Cancer's fragile yet strong nature.
White	Color	Represents purity, balance, and femininity. Ideally, Gemini would wear a white ribbon on their wrist for greater balance.

7 THE CHARIOT 7

Corresponding Tarot Card: The Chariot

Each sign has a corresponding tarot card that symbolizes some of its characteristics. In Cancer's case, it's the Chariot, which represents discipline, continuous progress in life, not dwelling on the past, and the desire to face new challenges. It gives them the strength to overcome the ups and downs of life and enhance their virtues.

Ritual for Cancer to Encourage Confidence and Perseverance

You'll need:

Cumin powder
Fine salt

METHOD:
Mix the cumin and salt and spread them around the corners of your house three days before cleaning. It will serve to get rid of doubts, negative thoughts, and insecurities, and allow you to be more steadfast about reaching your goals and objectives.

Cancer Compatibilities

Remember to check your Moon, Venus, and Mars signs in addition to the Sun sign.

+ (ANOTHER) CANCER
♡ ♡ ♡ ♡ ♡ ♡ ♡ ♡ ♡ ♡

They're both loving and dedicated, but their initial caution and mood swings can easily cause things to go awry.

+ LEO
♡ ♡ ♡ ♡ ♡ ♡ ♡ ♡ ♡ ♡

Although Leo's masculine energy may be attractive to Cancer at first, the lion's egocentricity will not be compatible with the crab's need for attention. This is a complicated combination.

+ VIRGO
♡ ♡ ♡ ♡ ♡ ♡ ♡ ♡ ♡ ♡

The calm and confident Virgo can delight Cancer, but they can also infuriate each other. Virgo may not be ready for the Cancer whirlwind.

+ LIBRA
♡ ♡ ♡ ♡ ♡ ♡ ♡ ♡ ♡

Two emotional and sweet signs, but Libra also undergoes frequent changes, which they resolve more independently than Cancer; at first it will be difficult to understand each other.

+ SCORPIO
♡ ♡ ♡ ♡ ♡ ♡ ♡ ♡ ♡ ♡

The emotional and sexual intensity of Scorpio can be attractive to Cancer, who will find great security in this sign. An obstacle is their tendency to be both somewhat spiteful and reserved.

+ SAGITTARIUS
♡ ♡ ♡ ♡ ♡ ♡ ♡ ♡ ♡ ♡

Sagittarius is, as a fire sign, a lover of risks and surprises, while Cancer is more about playing it safe. Their basic identities are very different.

+ CAPRICORN
♡ ♡ ♡ ♡ ♡ ♡ ♡ ♡ ♡ ♡

One of the best combinations. They are both domestic and traditional, and crave security. Capricorn will provide the structure and Cancer the emotions. They complement each other well.

+ AQUARIUS
♡ ♡ ♡ ♡ ♡ ♡ ♡ ♡ ♡ ♡

Cancer is the most emotional sign of the Zodiac. Aquarius is the most cerebral and guarding of their emotions. So Cancer's outbursts and Aquarius's lacking emotiveness can be difficult.

+ PISCES
♡ ♡ ♡ ♡ ♡ ♡ ♡ ♡ ♡ ♡

When guided by the heart more than by reason, the arguments between Cancer and Pisces will be frequent. But with similar emotional needs, the two can find great love with each other.

+ ARIES
♡ ♡ ♡ ♡ ♡ ♡ ♡ ♡ ♡ ♡

An initial attraction may arise, but their needs are very different. Aries's frankness can easily hurt Cancer, who will store away all the affronts until they can't take it any longer.

+ TAURUS
♡ ♡ ♡ ♡ ♡ ♡ ♡ ♡ ♡ ♡

They're both warm and loving, with a marked feminine nature. Although Cancer is more emotional, it can be a long-lasting and stable combination.

+ GEMINI
♡ ♡ ♡ ♡ ♡ ♡ ♡ ♡ ♡ ♡

Although as adjacent signs they can share positions, Gemini is independent and dynamic, and Cancer needs delicate attention and care. Both will have to compromise for the relationship to work.

THE MYTH THAT GIVES RISE TO CANCER:

Karkinos and the Twelve Labors of Heracles

One of the best known and most fascinating myths in Greek mythology is that of the Twelve Labors of Heracles (called Hercules by the Romans). Heracles was a demigod and one of the most famous heroes of Greece. He was the son of the god Zeus and the mortal Alcmene.

When Zeus proclaimed that the next child born in the house of Perseus would be king, Hera, Zeus's wife and goddess of marriage and home, jealous of her husband's promiscuous behavior, moved up Eurystheus's birth and caused Heracles to be born a few months later so that Heracles would not be king.

As an adult, under Hera's influence, Heracles killed his family. When he regained his sanity and saw the atrocity he had committed, he decided to go into exile. His brother Iphicles encouraged him to seek advice from the oracle of Delphi, who said, "Handsome Heracles, to redeem yourself from the barbarity you have committed, you will have to carry out the feats indicated by your archenemy Eurystheus."

These feats are known as the Twelve Labors of Heracles. Depending on the version of the myth, they vary slightly, but the list frequently includes the following:

1. Kill the Nemean lion.
2. Kill the Lernaean Hydra or the crab Karkinos (origin of the constellations Hydra and Cancer).
3. Capture the Ceryneian hind.
4. Capture the wild Erymanthian boar alive.
5. Clean the Augean stables in just one day.
6. Hunt the Stymphalian birds.
7. Tame the Cretan bull.
8. Steal the mares of Diomedes.
9. Steal Hippolyta's girdle.
10. Steal Geryon's cattle.
11. Steal the golden apples from the Garden of the Hesperides.
12. Kidnap Cerberus, the dog from the underworld, and take him to the king.

The constellation Cancer refers to one of the Twelve Labors of Heracles, although an extended version of this labor directs Heracles to eliminate the Hydra of Lerna. The Hydra is a mythological sea serpent with one, three, five, or even hundreds of heads, depending on the myth's version (its constellation is very close to Cancer; see the maps on pages 12–13).

This monster had the ability to regenerate two heads for each one it lost. The Disney movie *Hercules* refers to the Hydra story (although it's not too faithful to the myth of Heracles/Hercules and his Twelve Labors).

Karkinos, a mythological crab that inhabits the Lerna lagoon with Hydra, does not always appear in stories of this labor. Karkinos attacks Heracles when he's fighting the Hydra, an act that the goddess Hera rewards by turning it into a constellation.

Cancer Season

July 18

July 24

Leo Season

CANCER-LEO CUSP

July 18-July 24

Cusps are people born in the days immediately before and after the astrological seasonal change. People born on those dates may identify with traits of both the earlier and later signs. Depending on the rest of their birth chart, they may feel akin to their Sun sign or to the other sign close to their birth date.

The Cancer–Leo summit is also called the peak of drama, not because these people are very dramatic (although they are) but because they can be good actors and artists or otherwise dedicate themselves to the entertainment business. Furthermore, they're ruled by the Moon (Cancer's ruling planet) and the Sun (Leo's ruling planet), so they're people with a powerful emotional side who also have a magnetic and dominant personality. They can have a strong and unwieldy character.

Leo

JULY 23 – AUGUST 23

RULING PLANET: Sun

ELEMENT: Fire

QUALITY: Fixed
POLARITY:
Positive/masculine

FIFTH HOUSE:
Individuality,
originality,
impulsiveness

When talking about Leo, it's important to bear in mind that it's ruled by a male star, the Sun, the king star, which is represented by a lion, the ruler of the jungle. So it's no coincidence that Leos are people who shine with their own light. *Charming, flashy, sociable, passionate,* and *willful* are some of the adjectives that describe this sign. Leo's energy is characterized by being dominant—they're natural leaders with a lot of charm. On the more negative side, all this light can translate into arrogance, a magnified ego, or self-centeredness. These characteristics can be present in people with the Sun or with planets in Leo; the latter will present nuances that we'll explore in the following chapters, as well as with the rest of the signs. Among the fire signs, Leos are the most charismatic and ambitious.

LEO
Fire sign, fixed and masculine
July 23-August 23

VIRTUES: They are charismatic, loyal, energetic, strong, sociable, funny, generous, cunning, optimistic, brave, fast, enthusiastic, and leaders.

FLAWS: They are proud, superficial, self-centered, arrogant, domineering, authoritarian, frivolous, naive, rash, impulsive, and conformists.

FAMOUS LEOS: Jennifer Lopez, Kylie Jenner, Madonna, Mick Jagger, Daniel Radcliffe, Chris Hemsworth, and Charlize Theron

Constellation

Leo is one of the brightest constellations—all its main stars stand out at night, especially Alpha Leonis, also called Regulus or the Lionheart, located at the tip of the lion's nose or on the head. Other main stars include Denebola, Algieba, Zosma, Ras Elased Australis, and Adhafera. Leo is located west of Virgo and east of Cancer and very close to the Hydra (see the star maps on pages 12-13).

Leo's Ruling Planet: The Sun

As you will see in "The Astrological Planets" (page 103), the Sun is Leo's ruling planet. It's connected to the day, what's visible, the facets of our personality that we show to others. Therefore, Leos are people who like to go out, show themselves, and bring out the best in others with their optimism and enthusiasm. Leo is a common sign for people who are in the entertainment business. Leos are sociable people who enjoy motivating others through praise and who create an environment where everyone feels valued. They are charismatic and often reach their goals due to this natural charm. For this reason, at a young age, they achieve things effortlessly, which can result in impatient and affluent adults who are not used to striving to achieve what they want. Consistency is not a strong suit for Leos, but they're resourceful and unbeatable company.

Leo has Uranus and Saturn in detriment, Neptune in exaltation, and Mercury in fall. This will be explained in the next chapter (page 103).

How to Manage Leo Energy

Whether you have the Sun or other planets in Leo (see "The Astrological Planets," page 103), certain characteristics may apply to you. Let's explore how to make the most of this strong and dazzling energy.

As you may have already guessed, the biggest problem for Leos is wanting everything quickly and easily, because charisma is their main weapon when it comes to getting things done. Unfortunately, life isn't always a bed of roses, not even for Leos, so this sign can have real problems handling failure or rejection. In those instances, arrogance, intolerance, and selfishness can arise in Leo. Learning how to manage these types of emotions will be a challenge. Having earth-sign friends will greatly benefit Leos in this regard. Cultivating virtues such as patience and resilience will be easier if their birth chart has some position on the earth. In any case, Leos will find themselves in the right situations to develop these virtues. If they don't, their fire may eventually die down or diminish, and they'll become somewhat conformist and opportunistic.

Amulets for Leo

The most appropriate amulets for Leo are those that help them balance their most arrogant and carefree side, enhance virtues such as joy or confidence, and protect them against possible adversities.

Name	Type of amulet		Purpose
Gold	Precious metal		Leo's protective metal. In many cultures, gold nuggets were considered pieces of the Sun.
Amber	Animal origin (fossil)		Like the Sun itself, it provides confidence, power, and protection.
Citrine	White (semiprecious) stone		Enhances vitality and joy, characteristics already typical of this sign. It attracts good luck.
Tigereye	Golden to red-brown (semiprecious) stone		Balances the emotional side, calms the nerves, and drives away worries.
Sunflower	Flower		Symbolizes friendship and vitality.
Gold	Color		Represents power, self-esteem, self-confidence, and general splendor.

STRENGTH

Corresponding Tarot Card: Strength

Each sign has a corresponding tarot card that symbolizes some of its characteristics. In Leo's case, it's Strength. In the Tarot of Marseilles, and in most tarots, it's represented by a woman and a lion, which is the animal associated with Leo. It symbolizes willpower, mental strength, becoming strong, and standing firm in the face of adversity—skills that Leo will have to develop.

Ritual for Leo to Protect Themselves from Envy

You'll need:

White clay
Gold paint

METHOD:
Using the white clay, make a small sun about 1¼ inches in diameter (it doesn't have to be perfect, but the sun should be identifiable). After three days, paint it gold. Always carry it with you, as an amulet in your bag or pocket, to protect yourself from negative energies. It's important that you make the amulet yourself.

Leo Compatibilities

Remember to check your Moon, Venus, and Mars signs in addition to the Sun sign.

+ (ANOTHER) LEO
♥ ♥ ♥ ♥ ♥ ♥ ♥ ♥ ♡ ♥

Both are both bright and their emotional needs will be similar. The main issue: a possible duel of egos and frequent arguments. But the disputes are not spiteful and will be easily fixed.

+ VIRGO
♥ ♥ ♥ ♥ ♡ ♥ ♡ ♡ ♥ ♥

Although Virgo is shier and more analytical, and their focus can be beneficial for Leo to ground all that dazzling energy, the two will work better as friends than in a romantic relationship.

+ LIBRA
♥ ♥ ♥ ♥ ♥ ♡ ♡ ♡ ♥ ♥

Libra's emotional balance could be thrown off-kilter with passionate Leo, and the latter may find Libra too romantic or sensitive. The main issue will be respecting the relationship's boundaries.

+ SCORPIO
♥ ♥ ♥ ♥ ♡ ♥ ♡ ♡ ♥ ♥

This couple is compatible physically, but their emotions are another story—and that becomes their relationship's main issue. Scorpio needs an intense intimacy, while Leo is more superficial.

+ SAGITTARIUS
♥ ♥ ♥ ♥ ♡ ♥ ♡ ♡ ♥ ♥

Similar emotional needs, since both are sociable and love life. This couple shares the same way of living, enjoying, and loving, and can last a long time or leave an enduring memory.

+ CAPRICORN
♥ ♥ ♥ ♥ ♥ ♡ ♡ ♡ ♥ ♥

Each has a lot of character and their natures are very different, but Leo's charisma and Capricorn's ambition can make a formidable match. Very compatible in businesses, enterprises, or associations.

+ AQUARIUS
♥ ♥ ♥ ♥ ♡ ♥ ♡ ♡ ♥ ♥

Aquarius is philanthropic and Leo individualistic; both are sociable, changeable, and confident, resulting in a couple that's sure to turn heads. Leo will need a lot of attention from Aquarius.

+ PISCES
♥ ♥ ♥ ♥ ♡ ♥ ♡ ♡ ♥ ♥

Leo may find Pisces mysterious and attractive but also emotional and childish. So much sensitivity may not be to Leo's liking, who usually looks for a partner with a stronger character.

+ ARIES
♥ ♥ ♥ ♥ ♥ ♡ ♡ ♡ ♥ ♥

An extremely compatible partner. Aries has more of a temper, but both have the same way of dealing with problems and similar tastes and values.

+ TAURUS
♥ ♥ ♥ ♥ ♥ ♡ ♡ ♡ ♥ ♥

They can find great affection in each other. If they overcome their basic differences, it can be a lasting relationship, since Leo can find in patient Taurus their counterpoint and haven of peace. They are both strong and confident.

+ GEMINI
♥ ♥ ♥ ♥ ♡ ♥ ♡ ♡ ♥ ♥

The imaginative side of Gemini will drive Leo nuts. They both need a lot of independence and attention at the same time; this contradiction will be their main issue.

+ CANCER
♥ ♥ ♥ ♥ ♥ ♡ ♡ ♡ ♥ ♥

They share a certain sensitivity for aesthetics. But Cancer is more domestic and sentimental and requires that their partner provide them with security, while Leo may feel the need for more action.

The Nemean Lion, The Twelve Labors of Heracles

Like the constellation Cancer, Leo also comes from the myth of the Twelve Labors of Heracles (Hercules in Roman mythology). Since you've already seen this myth briefly on page 45, let's delve straight into the story of the Nemean lion.

It was the first of Heracles's labors, according to most versions of the myth. The labor consisted of killing the lion and stripping it of its skin, and it was no easy task: the animal—which had the population of Nemea on tenterhooks because it was terribly aggressive—had such a thick skin no warrior's weapon could pierce it and kill the animal.

The first time Heracles tried to kill it, he carried three weapons—a bow with arrows, an olive club, and a sword. Despite being a magnificent warrior, he failed to kill the giant cat. So he devised another strategy: he discreetly followed the lion to discover his lair, cornered him inside, and with his own hands managed to strangle him.

Next Heracles set out to perform the second part of the labor: skinning the lion. He tried multiple weapons, but he was unsuccessful.

Then Athena, goddess of wisdom, came down from Mount Olympus and secretly helped the hero. She disguised herself as an old woman and suggested, on the sly, that he use the lion's own claws to remove the skin from the lion's body. Heracles was skeptical of the old woman's idea, but he agreed to give it a shot. It worked.

Thanks to Athena's intervention, Heracles fulfilled the labor that King Eurystheus had asked him to carry out, and he prepared to take the trophy to Mycenae.

When the king saw Heracles wearing the animal's skin as armor, he was terrified. Rather than let him enter the city, Eurystheus arranged for Heracles to show the fruit of his labor from outside the walls. To serve as a reminder of Heracles's great achievement, the gods decided to turn the lion into a constellation: Leo.

The origin of the Nemean lion is not clear. Some versions claim that the lion fell from the sky, son of the god Zeus and the goddess of the Moon, Selene. Other versions say the lion was the son of the monsters Orthrus and Chimera. The Chimera was a monstrous being, described most frequently as having the head of a lion, the body of a dragon, and the tail of a serpent. In other versions, it's represented as a monster with three heads: one of a lion, another of a dragon, and the third, on the tail, shaped like a head of a serpent. Orthrus, on the other hand, was a monstrous two-headed dog whose owner was the Titan Atlas, condemned by the gods to guard the celestial vault for all eternity.

August 18-August 24

Cusps are people born in the days immediately before and after the astrological seasonal change. People born on those dates may identify with traits of both the earlier and later signs. Depending on the rest of their birth chart, they may feel akin to their Sun sign or to the other sign close to their birth date.

People born on the Leo-Virgo cusp attract attention for being outwardly "very Leo" (striking, sociable, charismatic), but when others get to know them more intimately, they're also organized, constant, and hardworking, characteristics more typical of the earth sign Virgo.

They have Leo's artistic and showmanship side, and the dedication and perseverance of the earth, so it's easy for them to succeed in whatever they set out to achieve, especially in the entertainment world. Furthermore, they love being in a relationship: they're very attractive, but they also crave stability.

Virgo

AUGUST 24 – SEPTEMBER 23

RULING PLANET: Mercury

ELEMENT: Earth

QUALITY: Mutable
POLARITY: Negative/feminine

SIXTH HOUSE: Routine, work, obligations, duty

Virgo is the most practical, methodical, and organized earth sign in the Zodiac. These people love the vibe surrounding the month of September—making lists, beginning classes, and planning for the future. Virgo energy is what motivates us to fulfill our obligations to ourselves and to society; therefore, Virgo people have a highly developed sense of duty. If you have a planet in Virgo other than the Sun, you'll see in the next chapter (page 103) how it affects you. And if you have the Sun in Virgo and you are a typically chaotic person (who doesn't thrive on organization), it's likely because you have a lot of energy in other planets or houses in your birth chart. This is how it works with the rest of the signs, as well. But pure Virgo energy is one of order, of light colors, of finding pleasure in small everyday details, and of developing values related to coherence and effort.

VIRGO
Earth sign, mutable and feminine
August 24–September 23

VIRTUES: They are constant, hardworking, organized, conventional, methodical, rational, professional, serious, reliable, sincere, analytical, stable, and perfectionists.

FLAWS: They are shy, reserved, critical, and not very innovative. It's difficult for them to recognize their mistakes. Some consider them boring, obsessive, impatient, irritable, and unsympathetic.

FAMOUS VIRGOS: Freddie Mercury, Beyoncé, Keanu Reeves, Amy Winehouse, Leo Tolstoy, and Hugh Grant

Constellation

The constellations closest to Virgo are Berenice's Hair, Libra, and Leo (see the star maps on pages 12–13). Its brightest star is Spica, located in the palm or spike carried by the constellation's woman. It represents the fertility of the fields and was a widely used symbol in the Middle Ages. The next brightest stars in the constellation are Zavijava, Porrima, Auva, and Vindemiatrix.

Virgo is the second largest constellation in the sky, after Hydra, and one of the oldest. It has been associated with various goddesses, such as Demeter, Athena, Themis, or Astrea, the last being the best-known version.

Virgo's Ruling Planet: Mercury

As you will see in "The Astrological Planets" (page 103), Mercury is Virgo's ruling planet as well as Gemini's. While Mercury in Gemini affects communication more directly, in Virgo it manifests itself in work dynamics, routines, and information as a means of individual and collective improvement. Up until the 1970s, Virgo was thought to be ruled by Mercury and the planet Vulcan, but then the existence of the planet Vulcan was disproved, so Mercury's rulership became unique. Thanks to this planet, Virgo stands out for their mental qualities: no detail escapes them, they're observant and usually seem quiet, but inside they're paying attention to everything that happens around them. They're very self-aware, both in their actions and in their words, and have a hard time admitting that they're wrong when they make mistakes or are in an argument.

Virgo has Neptune and Jupiter in detriment, Mercury in exaltation, and Venus in fall. This will be explained in the next chapter (page 103).

How to Manage Virgo Energy

Whether you have the Sun or other planets in Virgo (see "The Astrological Planets," page 103), certain characteristics may apply to you. Let's see how to get the most out of this kind of analytical and methodical energy.

As you may have already guessed, the biggest problem with Virgos is their inability to recognize mistakes, express empathy, and resist giving lectures. They can be know-it-alls. Activities like yoga can be beneficial to them as it joins the physical, spiritual, and mental and can help them get in touch with their emotional side and become more understanding.

Amulets for Virgo

The most appropriate amulets for this sign are those that help Virgos express themselves respectfully and confidently, and balance their more individualistic side, as well as those that reinforce work and professional relationships.

Name	Type of amulet		Purpose
Quartz	Transparent (semiprecious) stone		Protection stone par excellence. Amplifies positive energy and reinforces routines.
Peridot	Green (semiprecious) stone		Improves interpersonal relationships, and helps Virgos not be clingy.
Jasper	Reddish brown (semiprecious) stone		Gives courage and strength; very suitable to overcome shyness.
Brown agate	Brown (semiprecious) stone		Enhances the capacity for observation and analysis already present in Virgos.
Daffodil	Flower		Symbolizes discretion and resiliency.
Brown	Color		Represents modesty, work, earth, reason, stability, effort, adaptability, and maturity.

9 THE HERMIT 9

Corresponding Tarot Card: The Hermit

Each sign has a corresponding tarot card that symbolizes some of its characteristics. In Virgo's case, it's the Hermit. This isn't because Virgos never leave their homes and always reflect on deep issues (although they do); it's about enhancing the values of studying, meditation, and searching for knowledge from within themselves.

Ritual for Virgo to Enhance Decision-Making Abilities and Courage

You'll need:

Paper
Pencil

METHOD:
On the morning of your birthday, think about the craziest thing you've ever done that turned out well for you. Let that feeling wash over you, then make a list of the things you'd like to do if you were more daring. Put the list of actions in a visible place and try to fulfill them throughout the year.

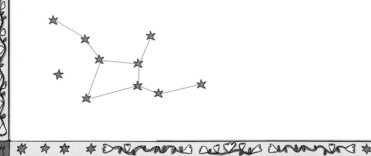

Virgo Compatibilities

Remember to check your Moon, Venus, and
Mars signs in addition to the Sun sign.

+ (ANOTHER) VIRGO
♥♥♥♥♥♥♥♥♡♡

They both enjoy order and routine. Watching movies at home under a blanket is a great date. This relationship may get a bit monotonous, but their needs will be similar.

+ LIBRA
♥♥♥♥♥♡♡♡♡♡

They share a sense of order, aesthetics, and well-decorated environments, but Libra is a sign that tends to be much more high spirited and flirtatious than Virgo, who is more serious.

+ SCORPIO
♥♥♥♥♥♥♥♡♡♡

Scorpio's determination and intensity can be attractive to Virgo, who will be fascinated by all that sensuality and mystery. Still, square Virgo can get overwhelmed.

+ SAGITTARIUS
♥♥♥♡♥♡♡♡♡♡

The carefree and open Sagittarius can seem unfocused and immature to Virgo, and Sagittarius can find the routine Virgo quite boring. They will have to work hard at their relationship.

+ CAPRICORN
♥♥♥♥♥♥♥♥♥♡♡

One of the best couples in the Zodiac. Strong physical attraction between the two, with a joint need for financial security, and great importance put on professional life and stability. Emotions are in tune.

+ AQUARIUS
♥♥♥♡♥♡♡♡♡♡

One of the most complicated couples in the Zodiac. Given Aquarius's desire for freedom and innovation and the more conventional mind of Virgo, this relationship will take effort on both sides.

+ PISCES
♥♥♥♥♥♥♡♡♥♡

The sensitive and dreamy side of Pisces is the perfect complement to Virgo's constancy. They will be able to develop original projects by joining forces. They captivate each other.

+ ARIES
♥♥♡♡♡♡♡♡♡♡

Aries's strong character, sociability, taste for luxury, and even their flashiness can be incomprehensible to the more modest and restrained earth sign Virgo.

+ TAURUS
♥♥♥♥♥♥♥♥♡♡

A very good couple. They both need security. Virgo is more analytical and Taurus tends to base their well-being on the sensory, but this couple can endure over time.

+ GEMINI
♥♥♥♥♡♡♡♡♡♡

Complicated combination. Gemini is a dreamer who is more open and talkative. Given their common ruling planet, Mercury, they work much better on a mental level as friends than as a couple.

+ CANCER
♥♥♥♥♥♡♡♡♡♡

Changeable Cancer, with their more emotional side, can be appealing to Virgo but can also be somewhat destabilizing. Patience will be required on both sides.

+ LEO
♥♥♥♥♡♡♡♡♡♡

Leo and Virgo have very different energies: Leo likes to show off and be admired, while Virgo prefers hard work and discretion. It will take a lot of effort to get along.

THE MYTH THAT GIVES RISE TO VIRGO:

Astrea

The constellation Virgo is the second largest after Hydra (see the star maps on pages 12-13). It represents a young woman with the fruits of the harvest in her hands. It particularly highlights the spike that she carries in her left hand (in the drawing in this book, it's a brightly colored flower). This element is formed around the star Espiga, one of its brightest, so this star is used to locate the constellation.

Many cultures associated the constellation Virgo with this young woman who symbolizes fertility and harvests. In Greek culture, it also represented young Astrea, the daughter of the god Zeus and Themis, goddess of divine justice. According to some sources, Astrea is one of the Titanesses. Astrea was entrusted by her mother with the task of helping administer justice among mortals; while the mother represents divine justice, the daughter personifies mortal justice.

Astrea was the last of the immortals to live in the underworld. Her father, Zeus, turned her into a constellation at the end of the Golden Age, a mythological era in which gods and mortals coexisted and where most of the Greek myths take place. The scale that forms the constellation Libra is located to Virgo's right. In some versions of the constellation, Astrea holds this scale that represents justice.

Astrea is also known for being the bearer of Zeus's rays and for being the only Titaness who was allowed to preserve her virginity. Since she was Zeus's ally in the war of the Titans, the god granted her this honor. There are several representations of this goddess and, therefore, of the constellation. In some versions, she appears carrying the rays of Zeus, in others she appears with a torch or the aforementioned spike or an ear of wheat. In some representations, she also has wings or a white habit or clothing, a symbol of purity and chastity.

The constellation Virgo is one of the largest in the universe. Its brightest star is Spica, but Auva, Vindemiatrix, and Heze also stand out. Additionally, the constellation Virgo is a cluster: the largest grouping of galaxies visible from Earth.

Virgo Representation

Typically, Virgo is the only Zodiac sign represented by a woman. For this reason, it's particularly associated with traditionally feminine characteristics: attention to detail and perfectionism but from a cerebral point of view, as it has Mercury (mind and communication) as its ruling planet and it's an earth sign (earth signs tend to be more rational and emotionally closed off).

Virgo Season

Sept. 19

Sept. 24

Libra Season

Leo

Fire

Fixed

Positive

Virgo

Earth

Mutable

Negative

Libra

Air

Cardinal

Positive

Scorpio

Water

Fixed

Negative

Sagittarius

Fire

Mutable

Positive

Capricorn

Earth

Cardinal

Negative

Aquarius

Air

Fixed

Positive

VIRGO-LIBRA CUSP

September 19– September 24

Cusps are people born in the days immediately before and after the astrological seasonal change. People born on those dates may identify with traits of both the earlier and later signs. Depending on the rest of their birth chart, they may feel akin to their Sun sign or to the other sign close to their birth date.

People born on the Virgo–Libra cusp are characterized by being delicate and considerate, wanting to make others feel good, and living in a harmonious environment. They are analytical but also highly sensitive and communicative, so others often trust them and tell them about their problems.

The greatest challenge that a person born on this summit faces is living and enjoying the present moment and not wasting energy on overanalyzing everything that happens around them and getting lost in details that go nowhere.

Libra

SEPTEMBER 24 - OCTOBER 22

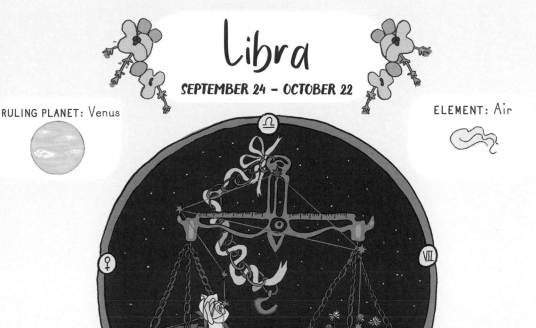

RULING PLANET: Venus

ELEMENT: Air

QUALITY: Cardinal
POLARITY: Positive/
masculine

SEVENTH HOUSE:
Couples, society,
contracts, friends,
enemies

Libra is the sign of balance and justice, as indicated by the scale that represents it. Yet this isn't a literal association, and it can lead to problems. Libras are always in search of balance: emotionally, socially, and even on a more superficial level. They take great care in how they dress and how they decorate their homes. They hate all things vulgar, excessive, or ordinary in any of its forms. This constant search for balance can affect their mood and, more intimately, their emotions—although, as you will see in the next chapter (page 103), this has much more to do with the Moon sign. Libras tend to prefer light color schemes and flirty decorative objects, and they love accessories. If you are a Libra and you do not identify with this description, you need to look at your birth chart. But we will get into that later (see page 152).

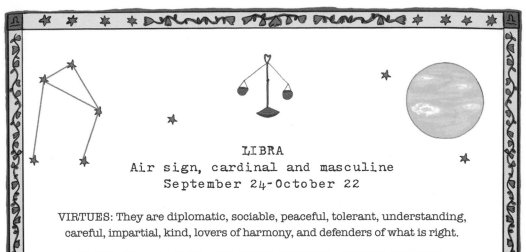

LIBRA
Air sign, cardinal and masculine
September 24-October 22

VIRTUES: They are diplomatic, sociable, peaceful, tolerant, understanding, careful, impartial, kind, lovers of harmony, and defenders of what is right.

FLAWS: They are moody, capricious, indecisive, complex, impatient, pessimistic, vain, superficial, influenceable, nosy, and dependent.

FAMOUS LIBRAS: Kim Kardashian, Pedro Almodóvar, Will Smith, and Julie Andrews

Constellation

This constellation is located between Virgo to the west and Scorpio to the east, and it's one of the least bright in the Zodiac. Up until Julius Caesar's time (first century BCE), Libra was part of the Scorpio constellation, forming the claws (as you will see in the following pages).

Libra's Ruling Planet: Venus

As you will see in "The Astrological Planets" (page 103), Venus is Libra's ruling planet as well as Taurus's. However, there is a significant difference between these two signs. As an earth sign, Taurus has a negative polarity, meaning it's an essentially feminine sign, and Venus is incredibly comfortable as a ruler there: it represents themes of a feminine nature, such as love, relationships, and pleasure. In other words, Taurus and Venus are in tune, which makes all these matters for Taurus flow naturally.

Libra, in contrast, is an air sign and, therefore, of positive or masculine polarity. With Libra, there's a tension between the polarity's masculine energy and ruling planet Venus's feminine focus. So although Venus makes Libras naturally attractive and they have a need for harmony, Libras tend to be more emotionally unstable and can have issues with self-image and self-esteem.

Libra has Mars in detriment and Saturn in exaltation. This will be explained in the next chapter (page 103).

How to Manage Libra Energy

Whether you have the Sun or other planets in Libra (see "The Astrological Planets," page 103), certain characteristics may apply to you. Let's see how to get the most out of this type of intense and passionate energy.

People with the Sun or other planets in this sign tend to play the role of mediators: they're the friend who wants us all to get along, and they're the perfect host, the person who creates harmony in the environment when entering a room. But for this reason, they can be too dependent and not express their needs clearly. This can lead to the occasional dramatic situation. It's key that Libras understand that expressing their needs or their real opinion, if done respectfully, doesn't have to lead to conflict. Trying to make everything harmonious is fine, but they should learn to break with that harmony, if necessary, so as not to become sad or depressed by not expressing how they really feel.

Amulets for Libra

The most appropriate amulets for Libra are those that help them remain emotionally balanced and contribute to attracting balance to all areas of their life (workwise, emotionally, spiritually, and financially).

Name	Type of amulet		Purpose
Jade	Green (semiprecious) stone		Improves both material and financial balance.
Topaz	Brown or gold (semiprecious) stone		Gives energy to its wearer.
Emerald	Green gemstone		Shares the properties of jade and is especially suitable for wearing as a polished jewel.
Aquamarine	Greenish blue (semiprecious) stone		Stone with powerful energy evoking the sea. Serves to balance Libra's more fickle side.
Hydrangea	Flower		Changing color symbolizes adaptability.
Pink and turquoise	Colors		Pink: related to Libra's feminine ruling planet, Venus. Turquoise: also related to Libra given its chromatic intensity; it symbolizes middle ground and balance.

Corresponding Tarot Card: Justice

Each sign has a corresponding tarot card that symbolizes some of its characteristics. In Libra's case, it's all about Justice. It literally represents justice and balance and truth, and, on its negative side, lack of decision-making initiative. They're all key themes in this sign, areas in which a Libra native will have to push themselves.

Ritual for Libra to Strengthen Resolve and Find Balance

You'll need:

White candle
Paper and pencil
Tea (your favorite one)
Glass jar with lid
Quartz

METHOD:
On a full moon, in a safe space, light the candle and surround yourself with the objects above. Think about what aspect of your life has no balance. Write down what you can do to improve the situation. Put the paper on a table. Place the tea inside the glass jar, close the lid, and set the jar on the paper, then place the crystal on the lid. Leave them in the moonlight.

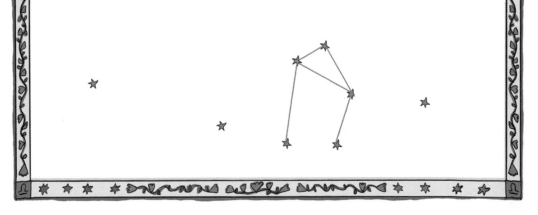

Libra Compatibilities

Remember to check your Moon, Venus, and
Mars signs in addition to the Sun sign.

+ (ANOTHER) LIBRA
♥ ♥ ♥ ♥ ♡ ♥ ♡ ♡ ♡ ♡

Despite their shared love for
order and aesthetics, their
indecisiveness and dramatic
ways of dealing with conflict
will mean they'll have to work
to understand each other.

+ SCORPIO
♥ ♥ ♥ ♥ ♡ ♥ ♡ ♡ ♡ ♡

Scorpio intensity can
overwhelm Libra. A somewhat
codependent relationship can
be established, as Scorpios
tend toward manipulation and
Libras can fall for their games.

+ SAGITTARIUS
♥ ♥ ♥ ♥ ♡ ♥ ♡ ♡ ♡ ♡

Sagittarius's optimism and
characteristic "letting go"
suit Libra wonderfully—
Libras can learn to make
decisions with them. Generally,
they work best as friends.

+ CAPRICORN
♥ ♥ ♡ ♥ ♡ ♥ ♡ ♡ ♡ ♡

Like other earth signs,
Capricorn is of fixed ideas,
and although both signs are
cardinal, Libra can find
Capricorn's ambition and
harsh character excessively
resolute and determined.

+ AQUARIUS
♥ ♥ ♥ ♥ ♡ ♥ ♡ ♡ ♡ ♡

This is a good couple. They
both need their space. But
Aquarius possesses a much
stronger sense of identity
than Libra, and Libra can get
lost in Aquarius's personality.

+ PISCES
♥ ♥ ♥ ♥ ♡ ♥ ♡ ♡ ♡ ♡

Both are soft and gentle souls.
They're good listeners, but
Pisces's emotional intensity
can throw Libra off-balance,
although there's a strong
attraction between them.

+ ARIES
♥ ♥ ♥ ♥ ♡ ♥ ♡ ♡ ♡ ♡

Although Aries has a strong
character, Libra will find
their initiative irresistible.
This couple may seem very
different, but they complement
each other well and are
sexually compatible.

+ TAURUS
♥ ♥ ♥ ♥ ♡ ♥ ♡ ♡ ♡ ♡

Taurus is stubborn and
even pigheaded, and Libra
changes their mind often, so
arguments will be frequent.
Nonetheless, they share a
taste for the harmonious
and beautiful.

+ GEMINI
♥ ♥ ♥ ♥ ♡ ♥ ♡ ♡ ♡ ♡

There's a strong physical
attraction between these two.
They're both sociable and
looking for light and pleasant
relationships; they both
dislike intensity.

+ CANCER
♥ ♥ ♥ ♥ ♡ ♥ ♡ ♡ ♡ ♡

The changeable Cancer, with
their more emotional side, can
be destabilizing to Libra. It
will take effort on both sides
for this to work. They have
difficulty communicating.

+ LEO
♥ ♥ ♥ ♥ ♡ ♥ ♡ ♡ ♡ ♡

Libra is sensitive to all of
Leo's sensuality and will fall
for their charm. But Leo has a
hard time staying interested,
and Libra's indecision can
overwhelm cheerful Leo.

+ VIRGO
♥ ♥ ♥ ♥ ♡ ♥ ♡ ♡ ♡ ♡

They can get along, but Virgo
is very clear about things and
Libra changes their mind
often; they can get on each
other's nerves in this regard.
It will take a lot of patience.

THE MYTH THAT GIVES RISE TO LIBRA:

Astrea or Julius Caesar?

The constellation Libra represents the scales of justice, which is carried by the goddess Astrea, also represented in the constellation Virgo.

Astrea was the daughter of the god Zeus and Themis, goddess of divine justice, and according to some sources, she is one of the Titanesses. Astrea was entrusted by her mother with the task of helping administer justice among mortals; while the mother represented divine justice, the daughter personified mortal justice.

Astrea was the last of the immortals to live in the underworld. Her father, Zeus, turned her into a constellation at the end of the Golden Age, a mythological era in which gods and mortals coexisted and during which most Greek myths take place. The scale that forms the constellation Libra is located to its right. In some versions of the constellation, Astrea holds this scale representing justice.

Astrea also known for being the bearer of Zeus's rays and for being the only Titaness who was allowed to preserve her virginity. Since she was Zeus's ally in the war of the Titans, the god granted her this honor.

Libra is a discrete constellation, with dim stars, located between the constellations Virgo and Scorpio. In some ancient representations, the constellation Libra is part of Scorpio—even in Greece it was sometimes called Scorpion's Claws. Libra became a constellation in ancient Rome by order of Julius Caesar and is the only constellation that doesn't represent an animal or a mythological man or woman.

Another symbol hidden in constellation Libra is the relationship between the scale and its ruler, Venus. It symbolizes this goddess's charm and her delicate balance: on the one hand, pure love; on the other, lust. This delicate balance embodies the essence of attraction and love between mortals, and it manifests in the natives of this sign.

Libra's Representation

Delving further into the scales' hidden meanings, their origin and connection to justice are found in ancient Egypt and its funeral rites. When a person died, they had to stand trial before the gods Osiris, Thoth, and Anubis. The deceased gave Anubis their heart, and he put it in one saucer of a scale. The heart represented the person's good deeds in life. In the other saucer, a feather symbolized the bad actions. If the heart weighed more than the feather, the deceased deserved eternal life. Later, the Greeks took the scale to represent justice, and the Romans added the sword and the blindfold to the goddess Iustitia, a representation that continues to this day.

Libra Season
October 19
October 25
Scorpio Season

October 19-October 25

Cusps are people born in the days immediately before and after the astrological seasonal change. People born on those dates may identify with traits of both the earlier and later signs. Depending on the rest of their birth chart, they may feel akin to their Sun sign or to the other sign close to their birth date.

People born on the Libra-Scorpio cusp are characterized by being ravishingly attractive. This is because they combine Venus's sensuality (Libra's ruling planet) with Mars's passion and fieriness (Scorpio's ruling planet). They're people who attach great importance to aesthetics and their personal image, but they have a scheming mind that tends to concoct plans and weave webs around their conquests. They can be involved in somewhat turbulent relationships because, on the one hand, they tend to idealize their partner, and on the other, they're attracted to mysterious people or those with a lot of energy (sexual and physical) from Mars. They experience strong passions.

Scorpio

OCTOBER 23 – NOVEMBER 22

RULING PLANET: Pluto

ELEMENT: Water

QUALITY: Fixed
POLARITY: Negative/feminine

EIGHTH HOUSE: Taboos, sex, intimacy, death, rebirth

Scorpio is a notorious sign: twisted, manipulative, and even a little sinister. This is also the sign with the greatest emotional depth, a great capacity for empathy, and an ability to rise from its ashes like the phoenix. Scorpio is the sign of deep transformation; they like to fully explore the complexity of the human soul. The spiritual, life and death, and the occult are subjects that will undoubtedly absorb Scorpio to a greater or lesser degree. This is one of the fieriest signs, since sex (together with an exploration of the subconscious, the hidden, and taboos) is one area in which Scorpios stand out. Their character is ensnaring and they're charismatic, but their charisma lies in the mysterious, the sexual, the forbidden. They can be prone to obsessions or toxic relationships. If you consider yourself a much lighter person than this and you are a Scorpio, create your birth chart (see page 152)—you likely have dominant planets in other signs.

SCORPIO
Water sign, fixed and feminine
October 23-November 22

VIRTUES: They are strong, determined, loyal, faithful, intuitive. They have the capacity for regeneration and are resolute, powerful, emotional, persuasive, cunning, and outsiders.

FLAWS: They are vindictive, controlling, ruthless, distrustful, jealous, temperamental, possessive, drastic, domineering, furious, manipulative, and vain.

FAMOUS SCORPIOS: Drake, Winona Ryder, Emma Stone, Joaquin Phoenix, Penn Badgley, and Björk

Constellation

The constellation Scorpio has been known since ancient times. It's a brilliant constellation, in contrast to the faint constellation Libra to its east formerly known as Scorpion's Claws.

Its brightest star is Antares, a vivid reddish star that's often confused with the planet Mars, hence its name: Antares means "opposite Ares," the Greek god of war comparable to Roman Mars.

Scorpio's Ruling Planets: Pluto and Mars

As you will see in "The Astrological Planets" (page 103), Pluto is Scorpio's ruling planet. However, Pluto is a relatively recently discovered planet. In ancient times, Aries and Scorpio shared Mars's rulership. Today, Mars is considered Scorpio's secondary ruling planet. The Plutonian issues include those related to the death of the ego, rebirth, the occult, and the intuitive on a subjective and subconscious level. In Roman mythology, Pluto is the god of the underworld and of death, the Greek equivalent of Hades.

Scorpio has Venus and the Moon in detriment. Pluto and Mars find their domicile in this sign. This will be explained in the next chapter (page 103).

How to Manage Scorpio Energy

Scorpio energy is one of the most difficult to manage. For Scorpio Sun people (and this can apply to people with other planets in this sign), the biggest challenge will be learning to let go. Scorpio energy is transformative; once mastered, it will help the person understand the deepest and richest aspects of human nature. For Scorpios, life can be painful, especially in youth, because they're unable to settle for the merely superficial. They're prone to obsession due to their tendency to delve deep into everything.

Scorpios are not into superficial relationships. They need emotional intensity to feel fulfilled and united with a person. The only way Scorpio can learn to let go and not obsess will be through experience. Life will give Scorpio the right people and experiences so that they can learn to appreciate this intense and personal part of experimentation. If you are Scorpio and don't identify with this profound energy, remember that creating your birth chart will provide more insight (see page 152).

Amulets for Scorpio

The most appropriate amulets for Scorpios are those that help them stay emotionally balanced and attract balance to all areas of their life (workwise, romantically, spiritually, and financially).

Name	Type of amulet		Purpose
Obsidian	Black (semiprecious) stone		Enhances vitality and influences libido and sexual emotions.
Malachite	Green (semiprecious) stone		Energizes its wearer so that they are not drastic and keep cool in stressful situations.
Red jasper	Brown-gold (semiprecious) stone		Relates to passion.
Iron or steel key	Object		Attracts material wealth and emotional and financial security. Scorpio should always carry it.
Peony	Flower		Represents desire and attraction.
Red and black	Colors		Red: color of strength, vitality, and passion. Black: color of mourning and death, of the end and the beginning.

Corresponding Tarot Card: Death

Each sign has a corresponding tarot card that symbolizes some of its characteristics. The Death card represents not only an end but a beginning. It points us to Scorpio's fundamental lesson: letting go of experiences, facing life in depth, and embracing the light and shadows, areas in which they will have to make an effort.

Ritual for Scorpio to Let Go

You'll need:

Matches
1 white candle
Incense

METHOD:
When a situation overwhelms you, strike a match, light the candle, then use the candle to light the incense, all in a safe place (like your home). Contemplate the smoke and think about what you want to let go of; when you're ready, let the incense burn down and tranquility take over.

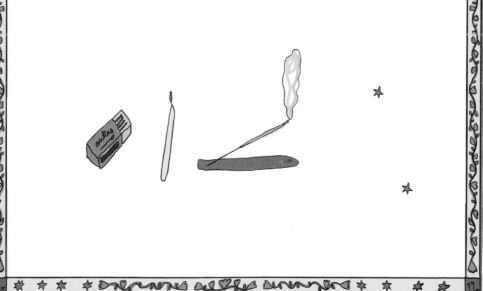

Scorpio Compatibilities

Remember to check your Moon, Venus, and
Mars signs in addition to the Sun sign.

+ (ANOTHER) SCORPIO
♥ ♥ ♥ ♥ ♥ ♥ ♥ ♥ ♡ ♡

Two very intense and sexual
people, but since they're
both irascible and somewhat
spiteful, problems can arise.
They must practice patience
and forgiveness.

+ SAGITTARIUS
♥ ♥ ♥ ♡ ♡ ♡ ♡ ♡ ♡ ♡

Although they can experience
funny moments together,
Sagittarius understands love
as something free and Scorpio
aspires to merge with their
loved one. It's difficult for
this relationship to flourish.

+ CAPRICORN
♥ ♥ ♥ ♥ ♥ ♥ ♥ ♥ ♥ ♡

They complement each other
wonderfully. Both can build
a stable relationship where
there is financial stability and
no lack of an intimate physical
and emotional bond. Beware of
jealousy and power games.

+ AQUARIUS
♥ ♥ ♥ ♡ ♡ ♡ ♡ ♡ ♡ ♡

Although there may be an
initial attraction, Scorpio is
a jealous sign. Aquarius will
either distance themselves at
the first sign of jealousy or
Scorpio will not feel confident
enough.

+ PISCES
♥ ♥ ♥ ♥ ♥ ♥ ♥ ♥ ♥ ♡

Both have a deep emotional
side and are very intuitive.
Pisces will feel protected,
cared for, and understood
next to Scorpio, and Scorpio
can find love in this sign.

+ ARIES
♥ ♥ ♥ ♡ ♡ ♡ ♡ ♡ ♡ ♡

This relationship can be
complicated. Aries's
impulsiveness is at odds with
the instinctive and mysterious
Scorpio. However, they can
encourage each other and be
very passionate.

+ TAURUS
♥ ♥ ♥ ♥ ♥ ♥ ♥ ♥ ♥ ♡

Complementary opposites.
Great attraction will arise
between them, but for Taurus
to feel good, Scorpio must
learn how to manage their
inner world; both must be
given some space.

+ GEMINI
♥ ♥ ♥ ♡ ♡ ♡ ♡ ♡ ♡ ♡

They're both resourceful;
they like to discover new
and original things. But the
excessive commitment and
dedication that Scorpio
demands in a relationship can
easily overwhelm Gemini.

+ CANCER
♥ ♥ ♥ ♥ ♥ ♥ ♥ ♥ ♡ ♡

A good couple. The two need a
lot of intimacy in a romantic
relationship, because the
attraction can be strong. Both
are temperamental, and they
must learn to forgive.

+ LEO
♥ ♥ ♥ ♥ ♥ ♡ ♡ ♡ ♡ ♡

They have strong personalities,
so arguments can be frequent.
The physical attraction
between these two signs is
undeniable, but the two are
very individualistic and will
collide.

+ VIRGO
♥ ♥ ♥ ♥ ♥ ♥ ♥ ♡ ♡ ♡

This relationship can be
emotionally stable, as both
feel protected and cared for.
Scorpio should try to use
their head more and Virgo
should stop being so critical.

+ LIBRA
♥ ♥ ♥ ♥ ♡ ♡ ♡ ♡ ♡ ♡

They can get along, but
Scorpio's jealousy may
overwhelm Libra, who doesn't
like mind games or high
demands. On a physical level,
they're quite compatible.

Orion and the Scorpion

Two versions of the same myth are known to explain the origin of the constellation Scorpio. They share two characters, Orion and the scorpion.

Orion is a mythological character who appears in many sources, although no ancient author tells the story of him in detail. Generally speaking, Orion was a great warrior and a giant. He was so big that he could walk on the bottom of the sea with his head jutting out above the waves.

One myth says that the giant Orion tried to rape Artemis—the virgin goddess of forests and hunting and protector of animals and nature—while she was hunting. To defend herself, Artemis asked a scorpion for help. It stung Orion, causing his death. The goddess, in gratitude, raised the scorpion to form a constellation.

The other myth says Orion was the son of the god Poseidon, god of the seas, and Euryale, princess of Minos. Poseidon gave his son the ability to walk on water. In this myth, there are two subversions: one says that Orion went blind and, while wandering aimlessly, a scorpion stung and killed him. In the second version, Orion, who was a great hunter, was hunting with Artemis and her mother, Leto. Partially to show off in front of the goddesses, Orion said that if he wanted to, he could kill all the animals on Earth, for he was a magnificent hunter. Upon hearing Orion, the goddess Gaea, protector of the Earth, became angry with him. But she also felt threatened and scared, so she sent a monstrous giant scorpion to finish him off. The scorpion killed Orion, and Gaea raised the scorpion as a constellation. The goddesses Leto and Artemis, impressed by the situation, raised Orion as a constellation, too, but placed him opposite Scorpio (see the star maps on pages 12-13). The constellation Orion shines brightest in winter but dims as summer approaches, while the constellation Scorpio brightens in summer and dims in winter; the two are forever at odds, as expressed in the myth.

Scorpio Representation

The scorpion appears in various mythologies, often referring to the dichotomy between its small size and apparent fragility and its lethal venom, capable of killing a large animal or even a person if it feels threatened. This meaning fits well with Scorpio's idiosyncrasies.

On the other hand, Scorpio's energy is also associated with the myth of Persephone: the innocent young woman who returns from Hades as a powerful and mature woman. It alludes to the process of transformation so frequently suffered by Scorpio women or those with the Moon in Scorpio in their youth. Assuming all the intensity and power of Scorpios instead of rejecting them is one of Scorpio's main challenges.

Scorpio Season

Nov. 19

Nov. 25

Sagittarius Season

Libra ♎
Air
Cardinal
Positive

Scorpio ♏
Water
Fixed
Negative

Sagittarius ♐
Fire
Mutable
Positive

Capricorn ♑
Earth
Cardinal
Negative

Aquarius ♒
Air
Fixed
Positive

Pisces ♓
Water
Mutable
Negative

Aries ♈
Fire
Cardinal
Positive

SCORPIO-SAGITTARIUS CUSP

November 19 – November 25

Cusps are people born in the days immediately before and after the astrological seasonal change. People born on those dates may identify with traits of both the earlier and later signs. Depending on the rest of their birth chart, they may feel akin to their Sun sign or to the other sign close to their birth date.

People born on this summit assume all the intensity of Scorpio's water and Sagittarius's spark of fire, giving rise to people with great initiative, rebelliousness, and character. They can also be extreme in their relationships: they will want all or nothing from those they love. At the same time, they can feel insecure, aware of all the love they need, and run away when they see that they may be vulnerable to suffering. They're spiritual people who combine the depth of Scorpio with Sagittarius's desire to explore new ideas.

Sagittarius

NOVEMBER 23 – DECEMBER 21

RULING PLANET: Jupiter

ELEMENT: Fire

QUALITY: Mutable
POLARITY: Positive/
masculine

NINTH HOUSE: Leave the house, travel, see the world, get out of themselves

Sagittarius is the most fearless sign of the Zodiac. Sagittarius's energy teaches us to share, open up, enjoy, give and receive, get out of our comfort zone, break boundaries, see the world, and reach out to achieve personal fulfillment. That's why Sagittarians usually have a restless nature, always wanting to learn and discover. They are sociable but not frivolous. Among the fire signs they're the most interested in philosophy and examining how other people think. A Sagittarius will always be willing to learn based on experience. They're optimistic people, with a passion for life. Nothing makes them happier than sharing what they have with their friends, enjoying themselves, going out, and traveling. They are open-minded, tolerant people who tend to have friends with diverse backgrounds, beliefs, and opinions. On the other hand, they can be somewhat scattered and avoid facing responsibilities. If you're a Sagittarius and you don't identify with this, remember that you must create your birth chart to see which signs dominate it (see page 152).

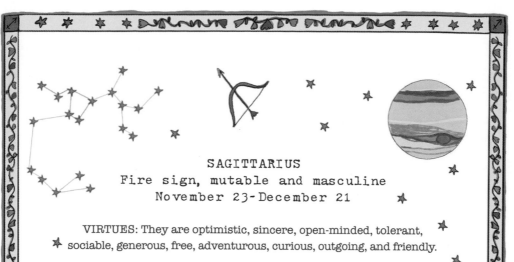

SAGITTARIUS
Fire sign, mutable and masculine
November 23-December 21

VIRTUES: They are optimistic, sincere, open-minded, tolerant, sociable, generous, free, adventurous, curious, outgoing, and friendly.

FLAWS: They are wasteful, exaggerated, impatient, irritable, irresponsible, eccentric, extreme, reckless, clumsy, inopportune, and disorderly.

FAMOUS SAGITTARIANS: Miley Cyrus, Britney Spears, Brad Pitt, Steven Spielberg, and Christina Aguilera

Constellation

The constellation Sagittarius is located farther south than others; therefore, observing from the northern hemisphere is complicated. Its name, Sagittarius, comes from Latin and means "archer." Its brightest star is Kaus Australis. It is surrounded by the constellations of Aquila, Scorpio, and Capricorn.

Sagittarius's Ruling Planet: Jupiter

As you will see in "The Astrological Planets" (page 103), Jupiter is Sagittarius's ruling planet. This is the equivalent of the god Zeus. As you've already seen while exploring other signs and their myths, Zeus was the playboy of Olympus: carefree, flirtatious, irritable—and that's being generous. Although Jupiter's planetary influence is less strong given its slow orbit, Jupiter represents order and authority. From a benevolent point of view, Jupiter's influence manifests itself by making Sagittarians extremely sociable and friendly. Furthermore, Jupiter's rulership is considered fortunate—those born under it will be likely to receive good financial news—but in return this rule also acts as an amplifier of negative effects.

Sagittarius has the Moon in detriment, the south node and Eris in exaltation, and the north node and Ceres in fall. This will be explained in the next chapter (page 103).

How to Manage Sagittarius Energy

Sagittarius energy is among the most lively, fearless, and adventurous in the Zodiac; however, due to their desire to live in the moment and enjoy the pleasures of life, Sagittarius people tend to spend excessively, and their carelessness and lack of planning and organization can lead to precarious situations. Sagittarius must make an effort throughout their life to organize themselves as much as possible. Unless their birth chart has positions on the Earth, Sagittarius should strive to create guidelines for that traveling energy—not to repress it but to make the most of it. For example, rather than spend on small, unimportant things, they can learn to manage their money and instead use it to take a class, do an activity they enjoy, or go on a trip. They can also learn to profit from the activities they enjoy the most, since a boring and monotonous job could extinguish the Sagittarius fire. The key to managing the dominant energies in Sagittarius personalities is not to deny that essence but to get the most out of it through self-defined guidelines.

Amulets for Sagittarius

The most appropriate amulets for Sagittarius are those that calm their mind, lift their spirits, and help them make good decisions, attracting fortune and giving them the peace and sanity to maintain it.

Name	Type of amulet		Purpose
Sapphire	Blue gemstone		Soothes their inner world so that they can make decisions as calmly as possible.
Opal	Multicolored (semiprecious) stone		Helps Sagittarius believe in themselves, reach their full potential, and give their best.
Lapis lazuli	Blue (precious) stone		Related to mental abilities and intellect.
Bay leaf	Plant		Attracts good luck and financial fortune. Sagittarians should place some bay leaves in a bag and carry them with them.
Carnation	Flower		Represents desire and attraction.
Violet	Color		Violet or its variants (purple, lilac) represent financial wealth and prosperity and also relate to the spiritual or mystical and learning journeys.

TEMPERANCE

Corresponding Tarot Card: Temperance

Each sign has a corresponding tarot card that symbolizes some of its characteristics. Temperance is associated with moderation, balance, and the right measure of things. It holds a fundamental teaching for Sagittarians, since these qualities are not innate and Sagittarians must acquire them throughout life.

Ritual for Sagittarius to Attract Material Prosperity

You'll need:

Charcoal
Bay leaves
Sugar
Matches

METHOD:
In a safe, open space, place the charcoal in a fire-safe container and light the charcoal using the matches. Add the bay leaves and sugar while repeating: "I want to get money and I will have money; with the bay leaves that I burn, I will attract money." Wait for the leaves to char completely, then throw the ashes into the air while repeating the phrase again.

Sagittarius Compatibilities

Remember to check your Moon, Venus, and
Mars signs in addition to the Sun sign.

+(ANOTHER) SAGITTARIUS
♥ ♥ ♥ ♡ ♥ ♡ ♥ ♡ ♡ ♡

These two people will fully
understand each other's
desire for freedom and will
respect each other's space,
but when it comes to finances,
they can be disorganized and
carefree.

+ CAPRICORN
♥ ♥ ♥ ♡ ♡ ♥ ♡♡ ♡ ♡

Although Sagittarius's wild
ideas can become reality with
the ambition of Capricorn,
they often misunderstand
each other when it comes to
love. Yet they can complement
each other well in business.

+ AQUARIUS
♥ ♥ ♥ ♥ ♥ ♡ ♥ ♥ ♥ ♡

They both love freedom.
Aquarius may find Sagittarius
somewhat carefree and
Sagittarius may feel Aquarius
is somewhat strange. They will
respect each other's space.

+ PISCES
♥ ♥ ♡ ♡ ♥ ♡ ♡♡ ♡ ♡

Although attraction can
arise, Sagittarius can feel
burdened by all of Pisces's
emotion. Still, both are
idealists and will fight to
live out their fantasy.

+ ARIES
♥ ♥ ♥ ♥ ♥ ♡ ♥ ♥ ♡ ♡

In many ways, they turn out
to be a good combination.
But both are impulsive and
irritable, they may argue
frequently, and Aries can
be somewhat jealous.

+ TAURUS
♥ ♡ ♥ ♡ ♥ ♡ ♡ ♥ ♡ ♡

Taurus, who above all seeks
stability and tranquility in
life, may run for the hills
when they see the roller
coaster that Sagittarius
intends to put them on
when entering their life.

+ GEMINI
♥ ♥ ♥ ♥ ♥ ♡ ♥ ♥ ♥ ♡

They are complementary
opposites. Gemini will always
be willing to teach Sagittarius
new things, and Sagittarius
will listen and put their
outlandish ideas into
practice.

+ CANCER
♥ ♥ ♥ ♡ ♥ ♡ ♡♡ ♡ ♡

The straightforward
honesty of Sagittarius can
hurt the sensitive Cancer.
Furthermore, Cancer
understands that their loved
one should be a refuge, while
Sagittarius sees love as more
open and less serious.

+ LEO
♥ ♥ ♥ ♥ ♥ ♡ ♥ ♥ ♥ ♡

A very good combination.
They both love to live the
good life, and they will be
compatible sexually. Problems
can arise from jealousy, as
Leo needs a lot of attention.

+ VIRGO
♥ ♥ ♡ ♡ ♥ ♡ ♡♡ ♡ ♡

Virgo's organized, practical,
and confident mind can
collapse with Sagittarius's
"disorganization," and the
latter can see Virgo as
somewhat boring and
monotonous.

+ LIBRA
♥ ♥ ♥ ♡ ♥ ♡ ♡♡ ♡ ♡

Libra needs a balanced and
safe partner, but one who
also respects their space.
Sagittarius brings Libra only
the latter and may find them
to be too sensitive.

+ SCORPIO
♥ ♥ ♥ ♡ ♥ ♡ ♡♡ ♡ ♡

They can have a good time
together, but striving for
something beyond the
physical is going to be
difficult, given Scorpio's
great need for intimacy.

THE MYTH THAT GIVES RISE TO SAGITTARIUS:

Centaurs

To explain the origin of the constellation Sagittarius we must talk about the centaurs. Centaurs are mythological creatures: half horse, half man. In the constellation, the centaur is illustrated with a bow, ready to shoot, representing Sagittarius's drive and momentum.

Yet there's no unanimous agreement that the constellation Sagittarius actually represents a centaur, despite that image having passed into the collective imagination.

No ancient myths mention a centaur shooting arrows. For this reason, it's believed that the constellation actually represents the satyr Krotos. A satyr is a different mythological creature, although somewhat similar to a centaur. Satyrs are half ram and half man. They live among the Muses and are cheerful and talkative, an image that fits better with the archetype of Sagittarius, since centaurs tend to be mysterious, imposing, and not very communicative.

Krotos was one of the satyrs who lived among the Muses, and two inventions are attributed to him in Greek mythology: applause and archery (although in other myths, they're attributed to other gods and creatures).

Therefore, it's possible to think that the origin of the constellation has more to do with a satyr than with a centaur. On the other hand, some people believe the constellation represents the centaur Chiron (not to be confused with the Chiron planetoid, a celestial body of second-degree astrological relevance that we'll explore later).

The centaur Chiron was the son of Kronos (god of time and father of Zeus, Poseidon, Hades, Hestia, Demeter, and Hera) and Philyra (a nymph of the waters). Centaurs were known for always being in a bad mood, wanting nothing to do with humans, and being terribly crude and insensitive. However, Chiron was an educated, quiet centaur and a master of multiple arts, such as music and hunting, and he instructed some of the most well-known Greek heroes.

The Origin of the Centaurs

As with most myths, there are several explanations about the origin of the centaurs. In one version, they're descendants of Centaurus (son of Ixion and Nephele, king of Thessaly and goddess of the clouds, respectively) and the Magnesian mares.

Centaurs in Greek mythology serve as a metaphor for the brutality of men and for uncivilized behavior. The mythical battles between men and centaurs are called the centauromachy, and it's a metaphorical explanation of how reason, culture, and law defeat brute force; similarly, myths about the Titans strive to convey the same message.

However, the centaurs Chiron and Pholus do stand with men in defense of civilization, art, and culture. And in astrology, Chiron gives name to a celestial body that we will explore in Chapter 4 (see page 136).

Sagittarius Season Dec. 19 Dec. 25 Capricorn Season

SAGITTARIUS-CAPRICORN CUSP

December 19-December 25

Cusps are people born in the days immediately before and after the astrological seasonal change. People born on those dates may identify with traits of both the earlier and later signs. Depending on the rest of their birth chart, they may feel akin to their Sun sign or to the other sign close to their birth date.

People born on this cusp are characterized by Sagittarius's strong desire to learn and experiment, combined with Capricorn's own ambitious mindset and hard work.

Additionally, Sagittarius's more wasteful and wild side finds balance with Capricorn's restraint and control, resulting in individuals with all the possible energy and curiosity yet always focused on the practical and concise.

On a more negative side, they're impatient individuals who can't stand people slower or less bright than themselves and tend to explode if they don't get what they want almost instantly.

Capricorn

DECEMBER 22 – JANUARY 20

RULING PLANET: Saturn

ELEMENT: Earth

QUALITY: Cardinal
POLARITY: Negative/
feminine

TENTH HOUSE:
Position in society,
status, vocation

Capricorn is the most ambitious and determined earth sign. They seek stability in life. It's important to them to acquire a good job and foster good relationships to achieve that stability. Does this mean that they're cold and calculating? Yes and no. It's not that they're cold, it's that Capricorn's personality is somewhat ironic and cynical, not for everyone. They tend to be emotionally closed off; this doesn't mean that they don't have feelings, rather that they feel everything to such a degree they don't want to be hurt. To gain their trust, you will need to show them your feelings through actions, which speak louder than words. They're very demanding, but that's because they're also very giving. Status is important to Capricorns. They're not social climbers, but they prefer to connect with people who are at their level in effort, dedication, and strength.

CAPRICORN
Earth sign, cardinal and feminine
December 22–January 20

VIRTUES: They are constant, ambitious, honest, loyal, confident, trustworthy, realistic, tenacious, persistent; strong decision-makers; and have an instinct for business.

FLAWS: They are selfish, cold, dissatisfied, melancholic, proud, inflexible, shy, apathetic, controlling, obsessive, and materialistic.

FAMOUS CAPRICORNS: David Bowie, Michelle Obama, Kate Moss, and Bradley Cooper

Constellation

Capricorn is located between the constellations Sagittarius and Aquarius on the Zodiac wheel. The other constellations near Capricorn are Aquila, Microscopium, and the Southern Fish (see the star maps on pages 12–13). Capricorn is a medium constellation. Although it's not one of the oldest, it already appeared in the second century CE as one of the most important and as a Zodiac sign. It's a dim constellation. The star that stands out the most is Deneb Algedi, which in Arabic means "tail of the goat."

Capricorn's Ruling Planet: Saturn

As you will see in "The Astrological Planets" (page 103), Saturn is Capricorn's ruling planet. Are you familiar with the painting *Saturn Devouring His Son* by Francisco Goya? Saturn for the Romans (or Kronos for the Greeks) is the father of many of the best-known gods (Zeus, Poseidon, Hestia, Demeter, Hera, and Hades), and of some of the most mythological figures, such as Aphros, Bythos, and Chiron. He is known for the myth in which he devours his children to avoid losing his power—although in the end, he's defeated by Gaea and Zeus. Saturn's rulership in Capricorn is manifested in issues related to power (if one knows the myth, this is an easy inference), status, one's own enslaving behaviors, work, restrictive rules and laws, structure, and indifference.

Capricorn has the Moon in detriment, Mars in exaltation, and Jupiter in fall. This will be explained in the next chapter (page 103).

How to Manage Capricorn Energy

Capricorn energy is closely related to ambition, tenacity, overcoming difficulties, and the fulfillment of goals and objectives, so everything that has to do with effort and dedication will practically come naturally. Yet, for Capricorns, life can be like climbing a mountain: an ongoing effort to move on, grow, and show themselves and others what they're capable of. They may forget that life has a lighter and pleasant side. In Capricorn's rigid dynamics, there's a small dichotomy: they don't want to lose control, but it's easy for them to feel that they can't take back the reins—so they leave situations up to fate (they're quite pessimistic). To stop this from happening, it's important that they include some fun and social activity in their day-to-day, but without "abandoning themselves." For example, they could set a day and time to talk with friends or choose a morning to spend with family; it's a matter of integrating those interactions into their routine.

Amulets for Capricorn

The most appropriate amulets for Capricorn are those that help them achieve their goals but also balance their emotional side and allow their feelings and desires to flourish, which helps them get what they want and also equalizes them.

Name	Type of amulet		Purpose
Onyx	Black (semiprecious) stone		Provides confidence, strength, and endurance to its wearer.
Hematite	Gray (semiprecious) stone		Drives away bad energies, reinforces optimism, and creates balance between the spiritual and the physical.
Smoky quartz	Red (semiprecious) stone		Strengthens concentration and memory, favors all mental processes.
Garnet	Dark red (semiprecious) stone		Brings courage and strength. When all seems lost, garnet helps Capricorn not lose hope.
Violet	Flower		Bright-colored with soft petals; delicate but strong.
Gray	Color		Neutral, solid, functional, practical. Represents the balance and seriousness characteristic of Capricorn; also represents intelligence.

15   THE DEVIL   15

Corresponding Tarot Card: The Devil

Each sign has a corresponding tarot card that symbolizes some of its characteristics. The Devil is the card associated with Capricorn—not because Capricorns are evil, but because it symbolizes that most of the time the chains they carry are self-imposed. Capricorn is a sign that tends to suffer due to its desire to achieve it all, and the lesson that this card brings is that we have the power to free ourselves from most ties.

Ritual for Capricorn to Ask for Protection and Calm

You'll need:

Sandalwood incense
Natural purple amethyst
Linden tea

METHOD:
In a safe and ventilated space, light the sandalwood incense, place the amethyst to its right, and prepare the tea. Repeat the following phrase seven times: "I want to be as calm as possible to carry out my purposes. I am strong and resilient," and drink your tea while the incense burns completely down.

 # Capricorn Compatibilities

Remember to check your Moon, Venus, and
Mars signs in addition to the Sun sign.

+ (ANOTHER) CAPRICORN
♥ ♥ ♥ ♥ ♥ ♥ ♥ ♥ ♥ ♡

This can make for a great couple, since they're both driven and share goals and ambitions. They seek security and stability.

+ AQUARIUS
♥ ♥ ♥ ♡ ♡ ♥ ♥ ♥ ♥ ♥

They share a rational side but are individualistic. Aquarius is more sociable and has wilder ideas, which can make Capricorn feel insecure and bring out their more controlling and jealous side.

+ PISCES
♥ ♥ ♥ ♥ ♥ ♥ ♥ ♥ ♡ ♡

Pisces will feel safe with Capricorn, and the latter can bring out their dreamiest and most creative side. They nourish and help each other through their weaknesses.

+ ARIES
♥ ♡ ♡ ♡ ♥ ♡ ♡ ♡ ♡ ♡

They have strong personalities, but they're very different. Intense competition can develop between them. Capricorn will find Aries irrational, shallow, and reckless.

+ TAURUS
♥ ♥ ♥ ♥ ♥ ♥ ♥ ♥ ♡ ♡

They're both earth signs, and their basic energies are compatible. Additionally, their differences will make them grow: Capricorn can learn to enjoy more with Taurus, and Taurus can learn to be more ambitious.

+ GEMINI
♥ ♥ ♥ ♥ ♡ ♡ ♥ ♡ ♡ ♡

Although Gemini's ideas and concerns can greatly fascinate Capricorn, their comings and goings and more casual idea of relationships can be quite unsettling. This makes for a good friendship.

+ CANCER
♥ ♥ ♥ ♥ ♥ ♥ ♥ ♥ ♥ ♡

They're complementary opposites. Cancer brings the home, the maternal; Capricorn, the material. They complement each other so that both are safe and at home.

+ LEO
♥ ♥ ♥ ♥ ♥ ♡ ♡ ♡ ♥ ♡

Capricorn is a sign that isn't carried away by superficial charm and flattery, but with Leo they could make an exception, if it weren't for Capricorn's jealousy—Leos are very flirtatious.

+ VIRGO
♥ ♥ ♥ ♥ ♥ ♥ ♥ ♥ ♥ ♡

One of the best couples in the Zodiac. They will inspire each other with confidence. The meticulous Virgo and the determined Capricorn can form an unstoppable duo.

+ LIBRA
♥ ♡ ♡ ♥ ♡ ♥ ♡ ♥ ♡ ♡

As an air sign, Libra may find Capricorn too dogmatic and inflexible. Libra can drive Capricorn up a wall with their changing minds and sensitivity. They will have to make an effort.

+ SCORPIO
♥ ♥ ♥ ♥ ♥ ♥ ♥ ♥ ♥ ♡

One of the best couples in the Zodiac. Both need a lot of stability and intimacy and are somewhat possessive, so they can develop a deep and enriching relationship.

+ SAGITTARIUS
♥ ♡ ♡ ♡ ♡ ♥ ♡ ♡ ♡ ♡

A complicated combination. Sagittarius enjoys life and loves discovering new things. Capricorn is more traditional and will not welcome Sagittarius's wastefulness.

THE MYTH THAT GIVES RISE TO CAPRICORN:

The Metamorphosis of Pan

When it comes to Capricorn-related myths, there are a couple of different versions of the origin of this constellation.

The first is found in the titanomachy: that is, the legendary war between gods and Titans, in which the Titans tried to seize power from Zeus and the rest of the gods to sow chaos and destruction. In this context, we find the demigod Pan, who was worshipped by farmers and ranchers. Pan was a satyr—half goat and half man. He lived with the Muses and liked to tease and chase them.

The Titan Typhon set out to destroy all the gods and began the war between the Titans and the gods. In the resulting chaos, Pan tried to escape to warn Hermes, so that he in turn could warn Zeus; Pan jumped into a river, intending to turn into a fish and swim out in a hurry, but the transformation did not go well and he ended up becoming a cross between a goat and a fish. Pan's warning came too late, as Typhon had already dismembered Zeus, so Hermes and Pan put Zeus's pieces back together so that he could wage war. In gratitude, Zeus raised Pan as a constellation.

A second constellation origin story is related to the cornucopia or cup of abundance. Rhea hid Zeus so that her father, Kronos, would not devour him (as he had done with the rest of his children, because Kronos was overcome with the fear that they'd grow up and take away his power). As a child, Zeus grew up in Crete with the nymph Amalthea, a woman with large golden horns on her head, like those of a ram. One day, one of Amalthea's horns broke off, and she filled it with fruits, flowers, and sweets and gave it to Zeus. In gratitude, he created the constellation Capricorn.

Capricorn Symbology in Astrology

The Capricorn character is very well captured and can be easily explained thanks to its representation. In Capricorn, we find a duality. On the one hand, the goat symbolizes Capricorn's desire to continue climbing, to be tough, strong, and tenacious like the mountain goats that endure inclement weather and their wild environment. The fish tail symbolizes the emotional, connecting Capricorn with water. This sign symbolizes how we can find the strength and security of the earth through our emotional side. Water nourishes the earth while emotions nourish the mind; to do away with the emotional side would be to castrate our intellectual side. Capricorns need to be in harmony and spend enough time with other people for this to work. This is a lesson that Capricorn must learn throughout life, as this sign is prone to relegate their emotionality so as not to suffer. It's difficult for Capricorn to understand that life doesn't have to be an obstacle course; they can let themselves be nurtured by water or emotions and the company of others, giving way to their true potential. People with a lot of energy in Capricorn or the tenth house in their birth chart tend to encounter dilemmas of this type throughout their lives, especially in adolescence.

January 17- January 25

Cusps are people born in the days immediately before and after the astrological seasonal change. People born on those dates may identify with traits of both the earlier and later signs. Depending on the rest of their birth chart, they may feel akin to their Sun sign or to the other sign close to their birth date.

People born on this summit are characterized by having innovative Aquarian ideas and the intention and perseverance of Capricorn to materialize them. Additionally, they're political people prone to extremes, since the seriousness and trust of the earth joins the winds of change, rebellion, and revolution that the air entails. They're also fixed in their ideas; empathy may not be their strong suit.

They will find it uncomfortable to be contradicted, and they can become dictator-like. They do not take relationships lightly, so they must be very careful when committing to someone—relationships aren't usually their priority.

Aquarius

JANUARY 21 - FEBRUARY 18

RULING PLANET: Uranus

ELEMENT: Air

QUALITY: Fixed
POLARITY: Positive/masculine

ELEVENTH HOUSE: Philanthropy, greater purpose, community associations

Aquarius has to do with everything innovative and breaking boundaries. It's a transgressive and original sign, but also tremendously rational and independent. Aquariuses are proud of being the black sheep and having a lot of personality. They are the first to follow trends—or are the ones who create them. Nevertheless, they tend to bet more on the collective good than on the individual; in other words, they're probably the first to join a political movement, an NGO, or a labor union, but when it comes to helping specific people or situations, they can be individualistic. They're self-reliant and detached people, so their attitude to someone's issue may be "If I can do it alone, you should, too." They are decisive and need alone time, although paradoxically they're also very sociable and outgoing. Their independence is often confused with a lack of empathy or feelings, but in reality, they possess deep emotions and high values.

AQUARIUS
Air sign, fixed and masculine
January 21-February 18

VIRTUES: They are innovative, rebellious, original, rational, decisive, analytical, philanthropic, tolerant, persevering, creative, and fun.

FLAWS: They are capricious, disconcerting, opportunistic, defiant, egotistical, eccentric, contradictory, radical, changeable, and complex.

FAMOUS AQUARIUSES: Mozart, James Dean, Cristiano Ronaldo, Shakira, and Paris Hilton

Constellation

Aquarius is one of the largest constellations in the Zodiac. It's located in the part of the sky called the Sea because it contains several constellations related to water: Cetus, Dolphin, Pisces, and Eridanus (see the star maps on pages 12–13). Its brightest star is Sadalsuud.

Aquarius's Ruling Planet: Uranus (and Saturn)

As you will see in "The Astrological Planets" (page 103), Uranus is Aquarius's ruling planet. Uranus rules everything related to rebellion, art, innovation, originality, and unique ideas. It's also related to progress, technology, and ideals. Likewise, it's associated with breaking down structures. Therefore, Aquarius assumes all these traits and manifests itself as the most rebellious and original sign of the entire Zodiac.

In mythology, Uranus represented the sky and was the husband of Gaea, goddess of the earth. He was one of the primeval Titans, father of many of the main Titans and gods, including the aforementioned Kronos, who in turn was the father of important gods. Aquarius's second ruler is Saturn; similar qualities apply to them as to Capricorns (rational, secure, and structured).

Aquarius has the Sun in detriment, Pluto in exaltation, and Neptune in fall. This will be explained in the next chapter (page 103).

How to Manage Aquarius Energy

Aquarius is one of the most (if not *the* most) complex and contradictory signs of the Zodiac. It's innovative, original, and rebellious but also rational and practical. Aquarius natives can suffer their greatest difficulties in the emotional area. They're very detached; they'll need a partner who respects their space and independence. On the other hand, they're sociable, likable, and friendly, even as they need periods of strict solitude.

Aquarius must develop their sense of empathy. Although they worry about issues such as equality or social justice, they're inconsiderate when it comes to other people's feelings. They tend to rationalize their emotions, which is why they find emotional or sentimental people difficult to understand. Inside the heart of an Aquarius is a longing for stability, and that's why they fear that other people will upset their balance. Faced with the possibility of being intimate with someone, they can become cold and distant for no apparent reason, but that's because they fear being vulnerable.

Amulets for Aquarius

The most appropriate amulets for Aquarius are those that connect them with their emotional nature. They bear strong associations with elements and themes from the myth retold on page 94.

Name	Type of amulet		Purpose
Turquoise	Blue-green (semiprecious) stone		Aquarius's good-luck charm. Most effective in its raw form.
Sapphire	Blue gemstone		Brings serenity and calm when making decisions.
Evil eye	Blue crystal		Helps prevent envy and bad feelings from enemies or false friends.
Black tourmaline	Black (semiprecious) stone		Brings clarity. Appropriate if Aquarius needs to focus on a specific objective or goal.
Orchid	Flower		Symbolizes strength of character and originality.
Turquoise	Color		Related to Aquarius through its ruler, Uranus. Refers to creativity, to the global, to the collective. The rainbow is also related to Aquarius.

Corresponding Tarot Card: The Star

Each sign has a corresponding tarot card that symbolizes some of its characteristics. In Aquarius's case, it's the Star, since both Aquarius and the eleventh house are related to transcending the material and surrendering to the collective, to influencing society. Other cards also associated with Aquarius are the Magician (a novel and original person) or the Fool.

Ritual for Aquarius to Overcome Nerves and Indecision

You'll need:

Acrylic paint in different colors
Brushes
6 natural stones
Wooden box with glass lid

METHOD:
On a full moon, paint the stones, letting your intuition lead the way. Allow them to dry, then put them in the box. Store the box in a dark place, and when you feel nervous or indecisive, take it out and look at the stones while taking a deep breath; this will help you connect with yourself and dispel worries.

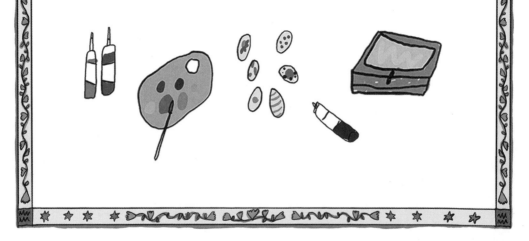

Aquarius Compatibilities

Remember to check your Moon, Venus, and
Mars signs in addition to the Sun sign.

+ (ANOTHER) AQUARIUS
♡ ♡ ♡ ♡ ♡ ♡ ♡ ♡ ♡ ♡

This is a fantastic couple. They both love their freedom and are creative and original. The union of two Aquariuses is undoubtedly a great combination.

+ PISCES
♡ ♡ ♡ ♡ ♡ ♡ ♡ ♡ ♡ ♡

Pisces needs complete fusion with their loved one: they're idealistic, believe in love, and have their feelings on display. Aquarius can hurt Pisces with their colder nature. There may be mutual attraction, however.

+ ARIES
♡ ♡ ♡ ♡ ♡ ♡ ♡ ♡ ♡ ♡

There's a strong attraction between these signs. They're sociable, dynamic, and somewhat reckless. It can be a passionate relationship, but raging Aries can overwhelm Aquarius.

+ TAURUS
♡ ♡ ♡ ♡ ♡ ♡ ♡ ♡ ♡ ♡

Although Taurus's stability can be attractive to Aquarius, Taurus will find them too eccentric with outlandish ideas. Aquarius can be overwhelmed by Taurus's attention.

+ GEMINI
♡ ♡ ♡ ♡ ♡ ♡ ♡ ♡ ♡ ♡

A very good couple. They're both dynamic, sociable, and outgoing. They are independent, but they will find each other fascinating. They both have an informal sense of relationships.

+ CANCER
♡ ♡ ♡ ♡ ♡ ♡ ♡ ♡ ♡ ♡

Cancer is emotional, has mood swings, and is quite dramatic—a mix that can blow Aquarius's cork. It'll take a lot of effort for this to work.

+ LEO
♡ ♡ ♡ ♡ ♡ ♡ ♡ ♡ ♡ ♡

They complement each other wonderfully. Leo provides creativity and individual ego, and Aquarius provides a more global vision. They'll have a lot of fun. The issue, in the long run, may be Leo's jealousy.

+ VIRGO
♡ ♡ ♡ ♡ ♡ ♡ ♡ ♡ ♡ ♡

They're both highly analytical and rational, but while Aquarius has a quick and agile mind, Virgo relies more on consistency and progress. They'll need patience for it to work.

+ LIBRA
♡ ♡ ♡ ♡ ♡ ♡ ♡ ♡ ♡ ♡

Libra is somewhat more sentimental and indecisive. Aquarius tends to get less overwhelmed, and Libra's constant ups and downs can make them lose interest in the relationship.

+ SCORPIO
♡ ♡ ♡ ♡ ♡ ♡ ♡ ♡ ♡ ♡

Unique and mysterious, Scorpio needs a great deal of emotional intensity, while intensity scares Aquarius.

+ SAGITTARIUS
♡ ♡ ♡ ♡ ♡ ♡ ♡ ♡ ♡ ♡

They're free, independent souls eager to discover everything new and unexpected, but Sagittarius's irresponsibility can get on square Aquarius's nerves.

+ CAPRICORN
♡ ♡ ♡ ♡ ♡ ♡ ♡ ♡ ♡ ♡

Despite being both rational and individualistic, Capricorn needs a lot of stability and commitment and is somewhat jealous, qualities that Aquarius will find tedious.

THE MYTH THAT GIVES RISE TO AQUARIUS:

Ganymede, the Cupbearer of the Gods

The constellation Aquarius is one that other civilizations, such as the Egyptians and Sumerians, observed in the sky before the Greeks. Yet they all saw in this constellation a water carrier, a water bearer, or a vessel pouring water. For the Egyptians, it represented the rising of the Nile and the origin of life; for the Sumerians, it referred to the god and origin of life, Anh.

In the Greek myth, the protagonists are the god Zeus and the charming Ganymede, the handsomest young man in the world. He was also the prince of Troy, which was no small thing. Zeus, of course, took a liking to the young man. While Ganymede was in the field one day, an eagle kidnapped him and took him to Mount Olympus. The bird was Zeus, transformed. Once they arrived at the place where the gods lived, Zeus entrusted Ganymede with the task of being the cupbearer for all the gods. To compensate Ganymede's father for the abduction of his only beloved son and heir, Zeus gave him a series of presents, among which were immortal white horses. To further fix the situation, Zeus dedicated the constellation Aquarius to Ganymede, which represented him pouring water from a jar. Even as a cupbearer, Ganymede seems to have found living on Olympus with the gods satisfactory, and he became one of Zeus's most loyal servants.

The constellation Aquarius is accompanied by that of the Eagle (see the star maps on pages 12–13); once again, Zeus gives the abductee a constellation in the shape of the animal he used to kidnap him (remember the constellation Taurus and the abduction of Europa, page 31).

Aquarius Symbology in Astrology

Although Aquarius is an air sign and Capricorn is an earth sign, both are indirectly related to water. While Capricorn's fish tail symbolizes that water nourishes and fortifies the earth (emotion reinforces logic, and reason does not cloud it), in Aquarius, water symbolizes something different: change. The constellation's water carrier bears a vessel from which water falls to the ground, revolutionizing it, moving it, and changing it.

On the one hand, this represents the rebellious and restless nature of Aquarius, their dynamic personality and connection with resents that facet of Aquarius we've already mentioned: their inner turbulence. They're independent, yet they frequently seek innovation and novelty, and they feel trapped and stagnant. They find it difficult to let their emotions flow freely (like water in a vessel), and a lesson they must learn in life is to let their emotional side flow (in their own way), since they tend to be much more rational and practical. Aquarius is the penultimate sign of the Zodiac. Together with Pisces, Aquarius represents emotional maturity, a goal that is difficult for these two signs to reach for several reasons, but achieving this maturity will be the culmination of their lives and result in the acceptance of who they really are.

AQUARIUS-PISCES CUSP

February 17-February 23

Cusps are people born in the days immediately before and after the astrological seasonal change. People born on those dates may identify with traits of both the earlier and later signs. Depending on the rest of their birth chart, they may feel akin to their Sun sign or to the other sign close to their birth date.

On this summit, the most prominent characteristic is the desire to save and help people, both individually and collectively. Aquarian philanthropy meets Piscean empathy and emotionality, resulting in tremendously dedicated and considerate individuals. They're capable of sacrificing and giving themselves and their lives for a greater cause or a collective by taking an interest in humanitarian or political issues, and they leave a deep impression on whomever they cross paths with.

On the negative side, they can live so much for the other person, that, to some extent, they lose their own identity.

Pisces

FEBRUARY 19 - MARCH 20

RULING PLANET: Neptune

ELEMENT: Water

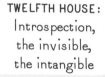

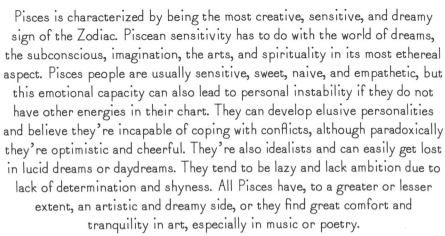

QUALITY: Mutable
POLARITY: Negative/
feminine

TWELFTH HOUSE:
Introspection,
the invisible,
the intangible

Pisces is characterized by being the most creative, sensitive, and dreamy
sign of the Zodiac. Piscean sensitivity has to do with the world of dreams,
the subconscious, imagination, the arts, and spirituality in its most ethereal
aspect. Pisces people are usually sensitive, sweet, naive, and empathetic, but
this emotional capacity can also lead to personal instability if they do not
have other energies in their chart. They can develop elusive personalities
and believe they're incapable of coping with conflicts, although paradoxically
they're optimistic and cheerful. They're also idealists and can easily get lost
in lucid dreams or daydreams. They tend to be lazy and lack ambition due to
lack of determination and shyness. All Pisces have, to a greater or lesser
extent, an artistic and dreamy side, or they find great comfort and
tranquility in art, especially in music or poetry.

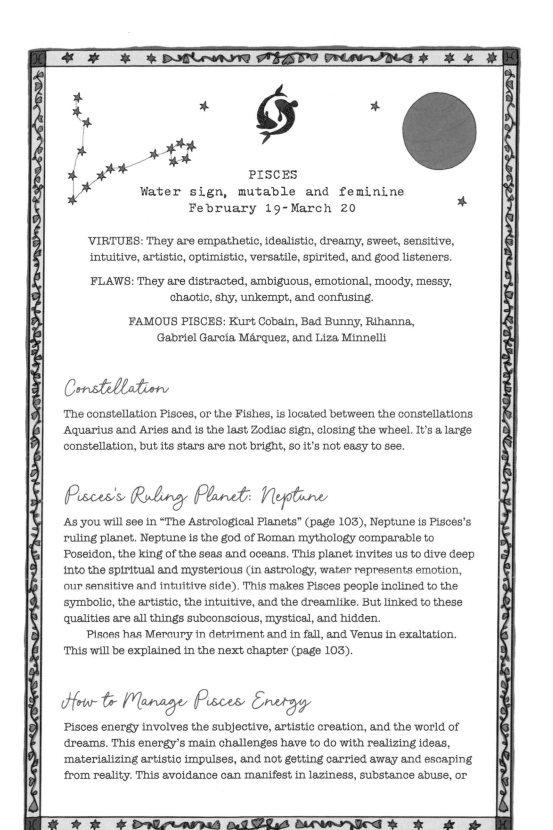

PISCES
Water sign, mutable and feminine
February 19-March 20

VIRTUES: They are empathetic, idealistic, dreamy, sweet, sensitive, intuitive, artistic, optimistic, versatile, spirited, and good listeners.

FLAWS: They are distracted, ambiguous, emotional, moody, messy, chaotic, shy, unkempt, and confusing.

FAMOUS PISCES: Kurt Cobain, Bad Bunny, Rihanna, Gabriel García Márquez, and Liza Minnelli

Constellation

The constellation Pisces, or the Fishes, is located between the constellations Aquarius and Aries and is the last Zodiac sign, closing the wheel. It's a large constellation, but its stars are not bright, so it's not easy to see.

Pisces's Ruling Planet: Neptune

As you will see in "The Astrological Planets" (page 103), Neptune is Pisces's ruling planet. Neptune is the god of Roman mythology comparable to Poseidon, the king of the seas and oceans. This planet invites us to dive deep into the spiritual and mysterious (in astrology, water represents emotion, our sensitive and intuitive side). This makes Pisces people inclined to the symbolic, the artistic, the intuitive, and the dreamlike. But linked to these qualities are all things subconscious, mystical, and hidden.

Pisces has Mercury in detriment and in fall, and Venus in exaltation. This will be explained in the next chapter (page 103).

How to Manage Pisces Energy

Pisces energy involves the subjective, artistic creation, and the world of dreams. This energy's main challenges have to do with realizing ideas, materializing artistic impulses, and not getting carried away and escaping from reality. This avoidance can manifest in laziness, substance abuse, or dependent relationships. To not fall into these toxic loops, the person with a lot of Pisces in their chart must work the Virgo–Pisces axis (see page 18). Virgo is the complementary opposite of Pisces, and Virgo energy is all about creating routines, daily work, and self-discipline. To get the most out of their Piscean side, Pisces must work on its complementary energy, the Virgo energy. By making the effort to maintain certain rules, order, and control, Pisces will be able to get the most out of their creativity, because these guidelines will help them and use all their emotional capacity both for their own good and for that of those around them. Along these Virgo lines, Pisces must also learn to set limits on people, since Pisces tend to lose themselves in others and forget about themselves. By setting boundaries, they'll be able to help others while still respecting their own emotional integrity and avoiding draining themselves.

Amulets for Pisces

The most appropriate amulets for Pisces help them maintain emotional balance, avoid entering toxic loops, and make the most of the talent and creativity that are part of their personality.

Name	Type of amulet		Purpose
Blue lace agate	Blue (semiprecious) stone		Helps to overcome shyness, providing calm and serenity to the wearer of this stone.
Sodalite	Dark blue (semiprecious) stone		Helps ground the wearer. Joins the logical with the intuitive.
Aquamarine	Greenish blue gemstone		Encourages calm and balanced decision-making.
Fish figure	Object		Pisces's lucky object. Jewelry in this shape brings luck to the native Pisces.
Dahlia	Flower		Symbolizes gratitude and empathy.
Blue	Color		Relates to the sea and emotions; usually related to Pisces through its connection with the subconscious.

18 THE MOON 18

Corresponding Tarot Card: The Moon

Each sign has a corresponding tarot card that symbolizes some of its characteristics. The Moon, despite being Cancer's ruling planet, is the tarot card associated with Pisces. It refers to their emotional nature and the dangers that this entails: Pisces, given their extreme sensitivity and imagination, can be dragged down by laziness and sadness if they don't learn to manage their emotions well.

Ritual for Pisces to Encourage Productivity and Drive

You'll need:

Piece of white quartz
Container with soil
Stick of sandalwood incense

METHOD:
On a full moon, bury the quartz in the container with soil, light the incense, and leave it all in the moonlight throughout the night. Say the phrase: "May the Moon purify this crystal, may the Earth charge it with good intentions, and may the wind of this incense give it strength." Before the sun hits it, remove the quartz from the soil and set it in your place of study.

Pisces Compatibilities

Remember to check your Moon, Venus, and
Mars signs in addition to the Sun sign.

+ (ANOTHER) PISCES
♥ ♥ ♥ ♥ ♡ ♡ ♡ ♡ ♡ ♡

Two Pisces together: perfect
emotional harmony, but their
sensitivity can make this a
chaotic relationship that
doesn't allow them to grow.

+ ARIES
♥ ♥ ♥ ♥ ♡ ♡ ♡ ♡ ♡ ♡

Pisces needs complete fusion
with their loved one; they're
idealistic, believe in love, and
carry their emotions close to
the surface. Aries is rough
and can hurt Pisces as well as
overpower them.

+ TAURUS
♥ ♥ ♥ ♥ ♥ ♥ ♡ ♡ ♡ ♡

Pisces will give Taurus the
understanding and sweetness
that they need, and Taurus
will give Pisces the emotional
stability necessary so that all
their virtues emerge and
they're calm.

+ GEMINI
♥ ♥ ♥ ♡ ♡ ♡ ♡ ♡ ♡ ♡

Like Aquarius, Gemini is
independent, but Gemini's
energy is much more anarchic
and creative, so they initially
have more in common with
Pisces.

+ CANCER
♥ ♥ ♥ ♥ ♡ ♡ ♡ ♡ ♡ ♡

Although on an emotional
and sexual level they're
compatible, they're both
emotionally explosive, so
drama is pretty much
guaranteed. They must learn
to be patient.

+ LEO
♥ ♥ ♡ ♡ ♡ ♡ ♡ ♡ ♡ ♡

They can experience
passionate moments, but
Leo's self-centeredness can
leave the Pisces empath
emotionally drained.
Complicated combination.

+ VIRGO
♥ ♥ ♥ ♥ ♥ ♥ ♥ ♥ ♡ ♡

They balance each other
wonderfully. They are
complementary opposites:
Virgo can help bring Pisces
to their full potential, giving
all the Pisces emotionality a
bit of structure.

+ LIBRA
♥ ♥ ♥ ♥ ♡ ♡ ♡ ♡ ♡ ♡

Libra's doubts and changing
mind can make Pisces feel
insecure and throw Pisces
a little off-balance. Still,
they're both idealistic and
romantic.

+ SCORPIO
♥ ♥ ♥ ♥ ♥ ♡ ♡ ♡ ♡ ♡

Their emotional worlds are
deep, and they'll be able
to establish a meaningful
relationship with each
other. However, so much
emotionality can consume
them a bit.

+ SAGITTARIUS
♥ ♥ ♥ ♡ ♡ ♡ ♡ ♡ ♡ ♡

They both get carried away
and are volatile. Sagittarius
needs a lot of freedom, and
Pisces requires intimacy. Two
very different worlds — it will
take effort.

+ CAPRICORN
♥ ♥ ♥ ♥ ♥ ♥ ♥ ♡ ♡ ♡

Capricorn is one of the most
serious signs, yet this can be
a rewarding union. They will
bring order to Pisces's
chaos, and Pisces will help
Capricorn open up and let go.

+ AQUARIUS
♥ ♥ ♥ ♡ ♡ ♡ ♡ ♡ ♡ ♡

They're both creative and
imaginative. But Aquarius is
a rational and independent
sign, and Pisces is emotional
and insecure, so it may be
difficult for these two to
understand each other.

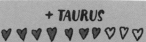

THE MYTH THAT GIVES RISE TO PISCES:
Eros and Aphrodite

The main characters in this constellation origin story are the goddess Aphrodite (called Venus by the Romans) and Eros (Cupid for the Romans). Eros was the son of Aphrodite and Ares (Mars in Roman mythology). Since Aphrodite is the goddess of pleasure and Ares is the god of violence and war, it's easy to imagine what Eros was god of: sexual attraction, sex, and love. The following origin myth is only one of many that exist. (Eros was a costar of the tale of Eros and Psyche, full of passion, jealousy, lies, and deceit—but that's another story.)

On a sunny afternoon, when Eros was a child, he and his mother, Aphrodite, were taking in the fresh air close to a river. She slept while the boy played next to her. Suddenly Aphrodite realized that the Titan Typhoon, one of the most horrible beings on Earth, was nearby, and it only was a matter of time before he found and hurt them. Quick as lightning, she grabbed her son by the hand and threw herself into the river. Aphrodite transformed into a fish, as did Eros, and they let themselves be carried away by the current, tied together with gauze so as not to be separated. They managed to escape from the Titan and, once they were safe, Aphrodite placed the gentle constellation of Pisces in the sky as a gift to her child.

An earlier origin story came from Assyria and dealt with Dercetis, or Atargatis, a half-woman, half-fish goddess. Here the constellation symbolized a single fish.

The Symbolism of the Fish

The fish has been a symbol in various cultures, many times related to the spiritual and mystical, as well as in astrology.

In Christianity, the fish is related to faith, with the premise that if you have faith, you will be rewarded with abundance (as in the parable of the loaves and fishes).

In China, fish are associated with marriage and love, as koi swim in pairs and are a common gift for couples.

In Scandinavia and Europe, fish are related to letting go, to enjoying and accepting life as it is, and to the ability to adapt.

In astrology, when representing the Pisces sign, fish are related to the hidden, the emotional, the sensitive, and the mutability of things; how we adapt to them; and our resistance (or not) to life's events. Fish give us the powerful lesson of letting things be as they are, as sometimes letting life flow means letting go and moving on, remembering the past as a valuable lesson, but not holding on to it.

Pisces Season

March 17

March 23

Aries Season

PISCES-ARIES CUSP

March 17-March 23

Cusps are people born in the days immediately before and after the astrological seasonal change. People born on those dates may identify with traits of both the earlier and later signs. Depending on the rest of their birth chart, they may feel akin to their Sun sign or to the other sign close to their birth date.

People (especially men) born on this summit have a marked personal charm. They know how to make people feel comfortable because they're cheerful and empathetic in appearance but also sensual and always up for a good time. Unless other positions contradict it, people at this summit tend to change partners a lot, leaving a brief and intense relationship to move on to the next one. They will have the charisma of Aries and the sweetness of Pisces, although they can be somewhat passive-aggressive.

4. The Astrological Planets

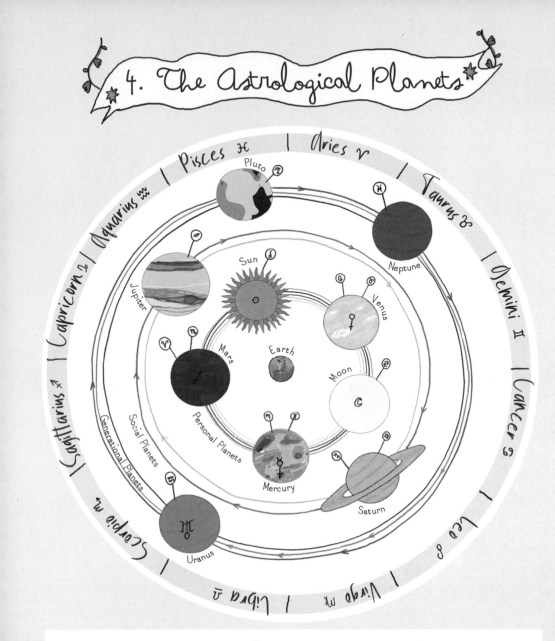

In astrology, every star near Earth is considered a planet. From our human point of view, it seems like the planets are moving from one sign to the next, traveling the entire Zodiac wheel. Thus the planets go, for example, from being in Pisces to being in Aries; when they retrograde, they appear to make the reverse journey (see page 105). The place that the planets occupy in relation to the Zodiac signs speaks of the energy available at the time, and it's very important when interpreting our birth chart. In addition to the astronomical planets (Mercury, Venus, Mars, Jupiter, Saturn, Uranus, Neptune, and Pluto) and the luminaries (the Sun and the Moon), we will examine some important angles (ascending, descending, midheaven, nodes, and Lilith) and other stars.

Classification of the Planets

In astrology, celestial bodies are divided into three groups, which affect different areas:

Personal planets: Sun, Moon, Mercury, Venus, and Mars. They have fast orbits and thus change signs every few days or weeks. They affect specific features of our personality, such as our way of communicating or loving, our interests, our emotions, or how we face an argument.

Sun	Moon	Mercury	Venus	Mars
Basic identity Self-image	Emotions Inner world	Communication Interests	Affection style Taste Sensitivity	Violence Rebelliousness Sex

Social planets: Jupiter and Saturn. They tell us how we can influence society and our environment, and how we should focus our personal development. Pay special attention to the houses (page 139) to interpret the social planets' meaning in our birth charts, in addition to the sign where they're located. They stay in the same sign for months or years. They're the ones that were known in ancient times and are the classic ruling planets.

Generational, transpersonal, or spiritual planets: Uranus, Neptune, and Pluto. They're an embodiment of modern astrology. They have a slow orbit (remaining in the same sign for years or decades), so we consider how they act in entire generations, marking historical and social moments.

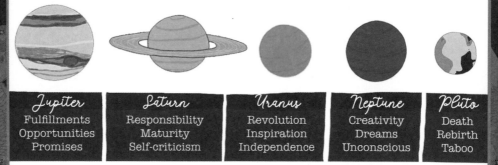

Jupiter	Saturn	Uranus	Neptune	Pluto
Fulfillments Opportunities Promises	Responsibility Maturity Self-criticism	Revolution Inspiration Independence	Creativity Dreams Unconscious	Death Rebirth Taboo

Angles and other minor stars: Later we will consider the influence of angles and positions between planets and points of the terrestrial geode, such as nodes, Lilith, ascending, descending, and midheaven, as well as minor bodies such as Chiron, Ceres, Pallas, and other asteroids. The ascendant, the Sun, and the Moon form a birth chart's three main positions.

The Astrological Dignities

What are they?
The relationship between a planet and a Zodiac sign is called a dignity in astrology; some dignities are more favorable or easier to carry than others.

Ruler or domicile: It's the sign where the planet is comfortable, where the energy will flow and will manifest itself comfortably.

Detriment or exile: It's the opposite of the domicile, and people with these positions will have a harder time being comfortable in that particular area.

Exaltation: This is the sign where the planet has the greatest influence. It will manifest as a powerful energy in that planet and position; it's favorable, and the native will have an easy time expressing it fluently.

Fall: The planet will be in fall when it's in the opposite sign of the exalted one. It's considered unfavorable; someone holding that position will find it uncomfortable.

	Planet	Ruler	Detriment	Exaltation	Fall
☉	Sun	Leo	Aquarius	Aries	Libra
☽	Moon	Cancer	Capricorn	Taurus	Scorpio
☿	Mercury	Gemini	Sagittarius	Aquarius	Leo
		Virgo	Pisces		
♀	Venus	Taurus	Scorpio	Pisces	Virgo
		Libra	Aries		
♂	Mars	Aries	Libra	Capricorn	Cancer
		Scorpio	Taurus		
♃	Jupiter	Sagittarius	Gemini	Cancer	Capricorn
		Pisces	Virgo		
♄	Saturn	Capricorn	Cancer	Libra	Aries
		Aquarius	Leo		
♅	Uranus	Aquarius	Leo	Scorpio	Taurus
♆	Neptune	Pisces	Virgo	Cancer	Capricorn
♇	Pluto	Scorpio	Taurus	Pisces	Virgo

Retrogrades

What does it really mean when a planet is retrograde?
We know that planets always rotate in their orbit in the same direction. But from the Earth's point of view during some periods of time, it seems like a planet moves backward. That's not really the case, but the optical illusion occurs because the planet is moving more slowly.

What astrological implications does it have?
A retrograde invites us to reflect and be introspective about the issue that governs the planet; it's nothing to worry about, but we may become less receptive. A retrograde is a period to consider how to better focus on the issue that the planet deals with. When the planet goes direct again (meaning it's no longer retrograde), it's time to put into action all the reflections that have taken place.

✸ The Luminaries ✸

In astrology, we refer to the Sun and the Moon as luminaries. They're considered the main and most influential stars in our birth chart.

The Sun represents the external, that which shines, the permanent, the physical, the form, our essence as a person, and our masculine side. The Moon represents the changing (like its phases) emotions, the inner world, the subconscious, the hidden, the energetic, and our feminine side. Since the Moon reflects the Sun's rays, in astrology the two are sometimes considered a single unit.

The luminaries symbolize our essential foundation as people. This association is connected to the origin of our culture as patriarchal. The masculine is related to the Sun and power, and the Moon to the feminine and the occult. Knowing this is key to having a complete view of this symbolism.

In my illustrated version of the luminaries, I've chosen to draw them as two women holding hands. It's not the traditional representation, as they're usually represented as a man (Sun) and a woman (Moon).

The Eclipses

What is an eclipse, and what is its astrological meaning?

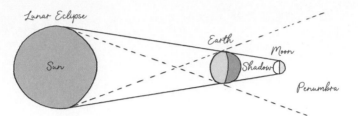

Lunar eclipses happen only during a full moon.

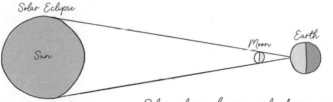

Solar eclipses happen only during a new moon.

LUNAR ECLIPSE: We notice that our feelings and emotions are altered; introspection and meditation are important. During a lunar eclipse, it's important not to recharge stones under the full moon.

SOLAR ECLIPSE: We notice that we have less energy; we're more secluded and less lively. Increased stress and dejection, tiredness, and fatigue are likely.

PREDICTIVE ASTROLOGY: RETURNS
In astrology, a return is a detailed forecast of our year based on our birth chart. Calculating it is complicated.

Solar Return

It marks a birth chart that's calculated at the precise moment in which the Sun is back in the same place as when we were born. It's annual.

Lunar Return

It marks the time of the month when the Moon is in the same place as when we were born. It's monthly.

The Sun

The reigning star in astrology tells us about our basic energy, which we manifest unconsciously; it's not difficult for us to integrate it because it is already inherent to us. Our Sun sign is the sign that the Sun was in when we were born; it's also known as our Zodiac sign. In men, the Sun and Mars are part of their masculine identity; in women, the Sun governs the traits they find attractive in other people and, of course, their basic identity.

The planets that form aspects with the Sun will influence our development. (You'll learn about the aspects in "The Birth Chart," page 152.)

The house where the Sun is located will indicate in which area you will stand out. (You'll learn about the houses in "The Houses," page 139.)

Ruler: Leo
Exaltation: Aries
Detriment: Aquarius
Fall: Libra

Retrograde: Not retrograde
Changes sign every: 29–30 days
Completes its orbit every: 365 days

The Sun in Each Sign

 The Sun in Aries is exalted; that is, Aries natives take to the extreme and manifest the influence of the Sun in all its intensity, which makes them fiery, risky individuals with a strong character. It's key for them to shine and stand out, and they can be somewhat inconsiderate if they're not taken into account. They like to be the center of attention.

 The Sun in Taurus usually gives way to calm individuals who enjoy life's pleasures without much regret. Bon vivants, calm, and presumptuous—but also pigheaded, stubborn, and slow to react to unforeseen events, which makes it difficult for them to form decisions and causes them to become stagnant or conform in some situations.

 The duality of Gemini is manifested in the Sun and gives rise to people who change their minds a lot and who find it difficult to maintain a fixed opinion. That also makes them adapt well to change, sociable, and liked by most people. They're friendly and laid-back. It's not difficult for them to fit into disparate groups or situations.

The Sun in Cancer denotes a somewhat irritable, emotional, traditional, and at the same time disruptive personality; in a word: contradictory. Cancers often tend to feel misunderstood, which can lead them to retreat into their shell a bit and not want to be vulnerable, especially due to childhood experiences.

The Sun in Leo is at home. Leos are often people with a natural charisma who are liked by the majority and who make and keep friends; they enjoy receiving compliments but also doling them out. They like to live comfortably, and they tend to do so mostly because of their people skills. They can be arrogant and self-centered.

The main feature of the Sun in Virgo is endowing its natives with a pronounced sense of observation and analysis. Virgos process things slowly, so no detail escapes them. They often look for ways to organize and classify their impressions, feelings, and belongings. Although they may seem messy, everything follows a logic.

The Sun in Libra is falling, which makes the natives of this position indecisive, not very independent individuals, who usually look for a template to follow. They often assimilate personality traits of close relationships from childhood, such as their mother (in the case of women) or older brothers. They will always be in search of harmony, and they avoid confrontation.

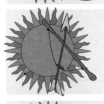

The Sun in Scorpio gives rise to somewhat mysterious people with profound feelings. Their ways are unorthodox. Other people may find them strange or not understand this sign's complex and deep inner world (the sign of the Moon will depend a lot on this Sun). But generally speaking, secrets, taboos, sex, and the occult are issues related to this Sun.

The Sun in Sagittarius is characterized by the search for new experiences, beliefs, and people. The Sun in Sagittarius will likely and especially manifest itself as carelessness and irresponsibility during their youth, but also as a desire to travel, leave their place of origin, and see the world. This will be highly nuanced by the signs of the Moon, Mars, and particularly Mercury (as well as by the rest of their birth chart).

The well-aspected Sun in Capricorn will give rise to confident, determined, ambitious individuals who know how to handle themselves well and safely in a variety of situations. When badly aspected, Capricorns can be lonely, materialistic, suspicious, emotionally closed off, and cold. Life can be a constant struggle for them, but it will depend on the rest of their chart.

The Sun is in detriment in Aquarius. This will result in individuals who are much less self-centered and much more collective. They're rational but idealistic, original, and creative. Above all, they are very difficult for others to understand, an issue that has a lot to do with this detriment from the Sun as well as their difficulty in expressing personal emotions.

The Sun in Pisces will give rise to people with all the sensitivity, adaptability, empathy, and inspiration of water, but also with its dispersion, lack of structure, and ambiguity. They possess great creativity and imagination, but if they're not focused and organized by positions on the earth, they find it difficult to translate their ideas into something useful.

The Moon

The Moon represents our emotional world, the inner world, how we feel intimately. It's related to the feminine and largely marks the relationship with our mother. In a woman, it's part of her feminine identity, together with Venus.

The Moon is also related to our instinct, our instinctual reactions, how we externalize what we feel, our idea of intimacy and emotional stability.

The Moon's house gives us information about what comforts us and what makes up our "safe place."

The planets that form aspects with the Moon will impact how we express our feelings and what affects us most on an emotional level.

Ruler: Cancer
Exaltation: Taurus
Detriment: Capricorn
Fall: Scorpio

Retrograde: Not retrograde
Changes signs every: 2–3 days
Completes its orbit in: 29 days

Topics related to the Moon that you will see in the following pages:
• The nodes (north node and south node)
• Lilith (the Black Moon)
• Moon phases and full moon rituals
• Each month's full moon

The Moon in Each Sign

The Moon in Aries will give rise to fiery, temperamental, and risk- and adrenaline-loving individuals with changing and intense emotions. They are direct and independent, and they take initiative in sexual relationships. They don't like compromises, which they interpret as ties. They demand a lot of attention and praise.

The Moon in Taurus makes their natives tend to feel good about what they have; they're satisfied, and they're often an emotional balm for those with a more restless inner world. On the one hand, they need their privacy and don't like being pressured; on the other, they want a loving and dedicated partner. They're usually emotionally stable and faithful.

The person with the Moon in Gemini rationalizes their emotions, is curious, and feels comfortable in anything new. They prefer to try different experiences and don't like feeling trapped or going deep into a single relationship, so they may come across as superficial. They're curious about living experiences.

The Moon in Cancer makes their natives stand out as loving, maternal, emotional, and sensitive people. They have a highly developed sense of empathy, so other people's emotions can greatly affect their own emotional stability and inner world. Their main virtue is protection, since they're family oriented and caregivers without even trying.

The Moon in Leo is usually a somewhat uncomfortable position, as Leo is ruled by the Sun. The Moon finds itself with desires to show itself to the outside world, which results in likable, dedicated people with noble feelings. However, because of this need to feel on the outside, they'll need external validation and can be very dramatic.

The Moon in Virgo empowers its natives with confidence. Impulsive and temperamental relationships can make them feel terrible. They can be a bit apprehensive and will need to analyze everything they feel. They'll find a home in people who are organized and who give them a sense of security.

The main trait of individuals with the Moon in Libra is the search for balance: they will not tolerate emotionally intense people, scenes of jealousy, control, or obsession. They need harmony to be content. They're emotionally indecisive, and they don't enjoy being alone (unless their Sun, Venus, or Mars contradicts this).

The Moon in Scorpio is in fall. It's the most complex Moon to handle for its native, with very intense emotions. These individuals are usually very intuitive, especially when it comes to other people's most negative facets. Once understood, this Moon gives unusual insight and depth. These people want to get to the bottom of things.

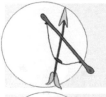

The Moon in Sagittarius provokes the need to explore, know, and see a multitude of possibilities, physically as well as emotionally and spiritually. If this search or adventure is not carried out due to circumstances or oppressive aspects with other planets, this person may feel dissatisfied. Even so, they will be cheerful, optimistic, and spontaneous.

The Moon in Capricorn is in detriment. These natives will need a lot of social, economic, and emotional stability to feel calm, and even then, they feel dissatisfied. They tend to base their well-being on the material, which can lead to somewhat selfish and greedy people. They're also responsible. They lack empathy (unless their chart is balanced with water).

People with the Moon in Aquarius want a lot of freedom and independence. They're somewhat peculiar in their needs, which can be disconcerting to their partners. They're not at all emotional and don't tend to bond deeply with others. They tend to project their emotional world outward and can be altruistic or disinterested.

People with the Moon in Pisces are the most sensitive. They tend to feel hurt easily; they go around in circles often and hurt their own feelings with their imagination, putting themselves in unrealistic scenarios, especially at the beginning of a relationship. They get excited easily, but they find it difficult to remain interested.

Lunar Nodes

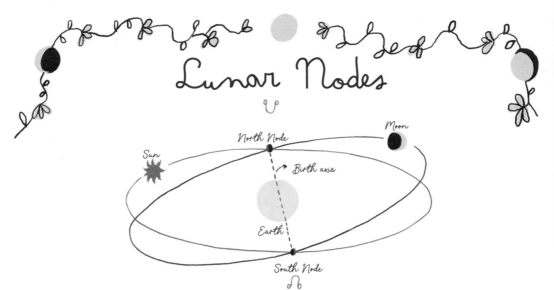

The lunar nodes, or "nodes of karma," show us which axis of signs we must work the most to develop our potential to the fullest and fulfill our purpose. Geometrically speaking, the nodes are the apparent intersection between the Moon's orbit and that of the Sun. The north node tells us what we must incorporate to grow, and the south node reveals what we must learn to let go of.

Characteristics of the Nodal Axes

ARIES NORTH NODE-LIBRA SOUTH NODE
You must try to be daring, to get out of your comfort zone. You must let go of complacent attitudes.

LIBRA NORTH NODE-ARIES SOUTH NODE
You must seek empathy, diplomacy, and meaningful relationships. You must let go of individualism.

TAURUS NORTH NODE-SCORPIO SOUTH NODE
You must seek balance between the spiritual and materialistic sides. You must let go of the need for control.

SCORPIO NORTH NODE-TAURUS SOUTH NODE
You must seek to be comfortable in innovation and uncertainty. You must let go of emotional secrecy.

GEMINI NORTH NODE-SAGITTARIUS SOUTH NODE
You should seek communication, patience, eloquence, and curiosity. You must let go of selfishness.

SAGITTARIUS NORTH NODE-GEMINI SOUTH NODE
You must seek expansion, experience, and wisdom. You must let go of indecision and doubts.

CANCER NORTH NODE-CAPRICORN SOUTH NODE
You must try to enjoy affection and seek love and compassion. You must let go of arrogance and loneliness.

CAPRICORN NORTH NODE-CANCER SOUTH NODE
You must look for savings, ambition, and strength of character. You must let go of oppressive emotions.

LEO NODE NORTH-AQUARIUS SOUTH NODE
You must seek self-confidence, self-esteem, and likability. You must let go of rationalizing emotions.

AQUARIUS NORTH NODE-LEO SOUTH NODE
You must look for creativity and the value of what is different. You must let go of narcissism.

VIRGO NODE NORTH-PISCES SOUTH NODE
You must seek order, constancy, and analysis. You must let go of ambiguity and laziness.

PISCES NORTH NODE-VIRGO SOUTH NODE
You must seek to be compassionate, supportive, and vulnerable. You must let go of overanalyzing everything.

Lilith

Lilith is a Judeo-Christian mythological character. She was Adam's first partner, whom God created as Adam's equal, independent and strong. When Lilith rebelled against Adam's authority, God banished her and, from Adam's rib, created Eve, a submissive and complacent woman (more or less, because as the story goes Eve made a mess with the serpent and the fruit of the Tree of Eden shortly thereafter).

In astrology, Lilith or Black Moon Lilith is a point between the orbit of the Moon and the imaginary line that passes through the Earth and joins the perigee and the apogee (the closest and farthest points from the Earth, respectively, of the lunar orbit). The sign where Lilith falls in our birth chart is a secondary position: in the case of women, it informs how they perceive their own feminine power; in the case of men, it reveals how they perceive the feminine power of women. It also tells us about the dark side of desire.

 LILITH IN ARIES
Moody and proud, sexual and even aggressive energy.

LILITH IN LIBRA
Contradictory position: the sexual impulse and the search for balance contradict each other.

 LILITH IN TAURUS
Passionate and possessive desire, determined and constant. Sensuality and money come together.

LILITH IN SCORPIO
Considered Scorpio's domicile; desire flows harmoniously. It's intense and disturbing.

 LILITH IN GEMINI
Contradictory. Desire increases with mind games. Ambiguity.

LILITH IN SAGITTARIUS
Expansive, free, and generous desire. Detached and jovial.

 LILITH IN CANCER
Carried away by passions. They don't separate the physical from the emotional and fantasy.

LILITH IN CAPRICORN
Bound and castrated by duty. What's desired is perceived as harmful and it's rejected.

 LILITH IN LEO
When sure of themselves, their desire springs from self-affirmation: I want it, I will fight for it.

LILITH IN AQUARIUS
Attracted to everything weird and original—desire is free from ties and intense.

LILITH IN VIRGO
Very selective and critical. It also manifests itself by being dedicated and helpful.

LILITH IN PISCES
Desire mixed with love, to merge totally with the beloved.

THE LUNAR PHASES

The phase of the Moon in which we are born influences us, just as it influences the growth of plants or the tides. The Moon phase in which we are born marks the available energy in relation to the lunar phases, it will explain the Moon sign, and knowing it can help us respect our energy cycles (rest when we need it and recognize when we have more energy). It's also of note that the Moon's cycle and the average menstrual cycle are the same (twenty-nine days), and many women's menstruation is in sync with the lunar phases. Since ancient times, farmers have related the phases of the Moon to the growth and pruning cycles of plants, and lunar cycles are also traditionally associated with hair growth.

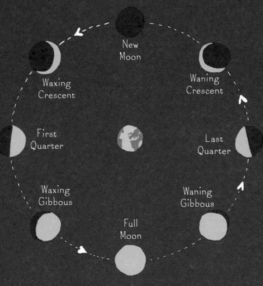

FULL MOON: Lots of available energy. People born under this moon are very nervous. During a full moon, people born on a waning or new moon may suffer from headaches or feel uncomfortable.

WANING: People born under this moon are dedicated to others, considerate, and empathetic.

NEW MOON: Those born under this moon possess greater intuition for the spiritual and occult and for emotional matters, and are capable of emotionally healing others through conversation.

WAXING: People born under this moon are open-minded and free—they like group dynamics and being in society.

THE THIRTEEN MOONS

Each year there are thirteen full moons, each marking a more energetic and powerful point on the calendar than the others. Those born under these moons are said to have a special purpose and powerful personal energy. Indigenous people named the moons after a crop or animal typical of that time of year. A series of rituals correspond to each moon, using specific plants that occur at the time of those moons. It also helped the gatherers remember what foods to collect at that particular time.

Wolf Moon
January

Cold Moon
December

Snow Moon
February

Beaver Moon
November

Warm Moon
March

Blue Moon
October

Pink Moon
April

Hunter's Moon
October

Flower Moon
May

Corn Moon
September

Strawberry Moon
June

Sturgeon Moon
August

Deer Moon
July

Full moons are associated with magic and female power.

Mercury

Mercury is the Roman god of communication, the messenger of the gods, and the equivalent of Hermes in the Greek pantheon.

Mercury rules our mind: how we communicate, what interests we have, our learning and organizational processes, and what topics or methods attract our attention the most—as well as with which people it will be easy to get along and with whom it will be necessary to make extra effort.

If you were born in Mercury retrograde, it'll be easier for you to communicate in writing than in person. Your way of expressing yourself may be unusual.

Retrograde: 3 times a year
Changes sign every: 1–1½ months
Completes its orbit in: 12–14 months

Ruler: Virgo and Gemini
Detriment: Sagittarius and Pisces
Exaltation: Virgo
Fall: Pisces

Mercury in Each Sign

MERCURY IN ARIES
Quick thinking and good at debating or even arguing, these people may be somewhat aggressive in arguments and may speak without thinking, hurting an interlocutor who is very sensitive. They're frank and direct when expressing their opinion and somewhat impatient and thoughtless.

MERCURY IN TAURUS
The thinking of people with Mercury in Taurus will be slow but certain; they need to be sure of things before deciding and they're determined and constant in study or work. They're sensible, but they have a hard time changing their mind. They're stubborn.

MERCURY IN GEMINI
People with Mercury in Gemini are curious and have a quick mind. They don't usually dive too deep into just one topic; they prefer to have superficial knowledge in many different areas, so choosing a single professional path can be difficult.

MERCURY IN CANCER

People with Mercury in Cancer tend to mix the rational with the sentimental, reality with fiction, and the objective with the subjective, so they're usually individuals with a talent for the visual arts, music, and poetry.

MERCURY IN LEO

People with Mercury in Leo are expressive, and their way of communicating is confident and somewhat dramatic or exaggerated. They manage to capture their audience's attention and are good speakers or actors.

MERCURY IN VIRGO

These people are analytical, meticulous, constant, and detailed and have a critical spirit. They're so detailed that they can get lost in the minutiae and avoid facing the big problems, focusing more on partial issues.

MERCURY IN LIBRA

Mercury in Libra gives rise to people who express themselves in an elegant way and who usually find the right words to describe everything with sensitivity and precision. They try to be impartial and see all possible points of view, which makes them indecisive.

MERCURY IN SCORPIO

People with Mercury in Scorpio go deep into the topics that interest them. They're irritated by people who think they're experts on a topic without being one, or who talk a lot and think little. Their mind is creative and deep.

MERCURY IN SAGITTARIUS

People with Mercury in Sagittarius are versatile and bright, but they don't usually delve into things; they prefer to have more of a general perspective. They tend to express themselves optimistically and openly but are somewhat inconsiderate.

MERCURY IN CAPRICORN

Their way of expressing themselves is pragmatic and cold; they're not interested in emotional arguments or things that they can't understand through reason. They may feel more comfortable working in a scientific field and are rigorous and firm in their ideas.

MERCURY IN AQUARIUS

The key words that define people with Mercury in Aquarius are creative, idealistic, unconventional, innovative, and even revolutionary. They love to experiment and this leads to unorthodox yet always interesting solutions.

MERCURY IN PISCES

People with Mercury in Pisces express themselves in imaginative and dreamy ways, and their tastes are often artistic. They may find themselves more comfortable expressing themselves in a creative manner. They get carried away by intuition more than reason.

Venus

Venus is the Roman goddess of beauty, love, and sexuality, the Greek equivalent of Aphrodite. Venus governs our tastes (both aesthetic and romantic) and our way of loving and relating affectionately. The house where Venus is located indicates which areas of life we feel most comfortable engaging in. The aspects with Venus denote what kind of people we like to associate with. If you were born on Venus retrograde, you may tend to overanalyze your relationships.

Retrograde: 2 times every 3 years
Changes sign every: 3 weeks–1 month
Completes its orbit in: 10–12 months

Ruler: Taurus and Libra
Detriment: Scorpio and Aries
Exaltation: Pisces
Fall: Virgo

Venus in Each Sign

VENUS IN ARIES
People with Venus in Aries enjoy flirting and the initial conquest period in a relationship, but it is difficult for them to maintain their interest over time. They're passionate and impulsive and can be somewhat emotionally inconsiderate.

VENUS IN TAURUS
People with Venus in Taurus are characterized by needing security in their relationships. They are calm and loving, but they also rationally look for a partner who doesn't cause too many headaches, likes to pamper them, and showers them with attention.

VENUS IN GEMINI
People with Venus in Gemini are known for being somewhat emotionally volatile and having strong attractions to people who seem interesting to them on an intellectual or mental level. It's difficult for them to break up or make drastic decisions.

VENUS IN CANCER

People with Venus in Cancer are characterized by their sensitivity. They may connect romantically with people who need protection or nurturing rather than choose partners based on mutual attraction.

VENUS IN LEO

The person with Venus in Leo can be loving and devoted, but they'll need (at the very least) for their partner to reciprocate in kind. If not, they'll quickly lose interest. They tend to be confident and enjoy flirting.

VENUS IN VIRGO

People with Venus in Virgo often rationalize their feelings and don't get carried away by romantic impulses or uncontrolled passions. They need security, but they're demanding, so they can tend to be alone.

VENUS IN LIBRA

The person with Venus in Libra will tend to seek harmony in their relationships above all else, which can lead them to not express their feelings openly for fear of creating a conflict.

VENUS IN SCORPIO

The person with Venus in Scorpio will experience intense loves and hates; they tend to feel hurt or disappointed easily but also can't resist magnetic people. Jealousy or power struggles may appear.

VENUS IN SAGITTARIUS

The person with Venus in Sagittarius tends to be an independent person who doesn't want to subject themselves to ties of any kind; they will be easily attracted to foreign or philosophical people who are also independent.

VENUS IN CAPRICORN

The person with Venus in Capricorn can be emotionally closed off; on the one hand, they don't hang out with just anyone (they need their space); on the other, they demand a lot of intensity, attention, and care in a relationship.

VENUS IN AQUARIUS

The person with Venus in Aquarius will flee from ties that bind and will be attracted to unconventional, cool, and extravagant people with whom they'll be able to establish a close bond. They're not jealous at all (if the Moon doesn't contradict this).

VENUS IN PISCES

The person with Venus in Pisces will be tender and devoted, besotted, and sweet. They tend to idealize their partners and therefore will be prone to disappointment. Also, it may be difficult for them to set limits, which they must learn to do.

Mars

Mars is the Roman god of war. His Greek equivalent is Ares. Mars fundamentally rules violence and sexual impulse. The sign of Aries will determine not only how we face a conflict but also how we develop sexually. If you were born on Mars retrograde, you will alternate periods of being very active with others of greater exhaustion.

Retrograde: 2 times every 3 years
Changes sign every: 2 months, approximately
Completes its orbit in: 2 years, approximately

Ruler: Aries and Scorpio
Detriment: Libra and Taurus
Exaltation: Capricorn
Fall: Cancer

Mars in Each Sign

MARS IN ARIES
The person with Mars in Aries isn't violent per se, but they are impulsive and active and have a lot of energy. They're not afraid to take the first step in a relationship, but they usually don't remain interested for long. Sexually, they will be fiery and passionate.

MARS IN TAURUS
The person with Mars in Taurus, if other planets don't contradict this, will be calm and avoid conflicts; their decisions will be thoughtful, and they will be steadfast if they set out to do something. Sexually, they're quite conventional.

MARS IN GEMINI
The main trait of a person with Mars in Gemini is curiosity: they're people who in the sexual field like to experiment and play. Communication with their partner will also be very important; sparks have to fly on an intellectual level.

MARS IN CANCER
People with Mars in Cancer go through the same situation both when facing a problem or arguing and when starting a relationship: they find it difficult to separate the emotional from the rational or physical; their decisions in any area are guided by the heart.

MARS IN LEO
People with Mars in Leo can be attractive, daring, funny, and impulsive. They like to be adored and recognized, but they can be quite proud. Sexually, they're passionate and affectionate at the same time.

MARS IN VIRGO
To make any decision, people with Mars in Virgo may overanalyze everything just a little bit. They can be somewhat shy both in love and physically. They need guarantees and a lot of confidence to loosen up and enjoy.

MARS IN LIBRA
The person with Mars in Libra will look for people who make them feel balanced, those who are refined and not too intense. They shy away from conflict, so they may not be entirely sincere with their intentions or needs.

MARS IN SCORPIO
The person with Mars in Scorpio will be sexual, attractive, fiery, mysterious, and charismatic and will stir up great passions. They tend to be confident people who choose their partners; they're determined and emotional.

MARS IN SAGITTARIUS
People with Mars in Sagittarius seek inspiring relationships; they're curious and want to live as freely as possible. They're also direct and somewhat impulsive. They don't usually seek commitment.

MARS IN CAPRICORN
People with Mars in Capricorn are confident, strong, and independent, but once committed they need a lot of attention, feel very self-conscious, and fear being rejected. They're traditional and determined.

MARS IN AQUARIUS
People with Mars in Aquarius are original and charismatic. They're attracted to the strange or different, and their behavior is quite peculiar. In relationships, they're unpredictable: they like to have fun but they don't fully commit.

MARS IN PISCES
Similar to those with Mars in Cancer, people with Mars in Pisces often mix heart and reason; they are dreamers and attracted to mystical or profound people. The emotional and the sexual go hand in hand in their case.

Jupiter

Jupiter is the Roman god equivalent to Zeus. The planet Jupiter represents sociability: how we relate to others and extend our horizons. Usually all people born in the same year have the same natal Jupiter. The house where it's located tells us in which areas we will seek to expand; the aspects will explain what things give meaning to our lives.

Retrograde: not every year (retrograde lasts almost 4 months)
Changes sign every: 1 year, approximately
Completes its orbit in: 12 years

Ruler: Sagittarius and Pisces
Exaltation: Cancer
Detriment: Gemini and Virgo
Fall: Capricorn

Jupiter in Each Sign

JUPITER IN ARIES
Those with Jupiter in Aries are self-confident, brave, bold, very willing to get ahead, and eager to go out into the world to discover and get to know who they are.

JUPITER IN TAURUS
People with Jupiter in Taurus will seek stability through the material as well as the mental or intellectual. Their values tend to be more conservative. Enjoying the sensory is important to them.

JUPITER IN GEMINI
For people with Jupiter in Gemini, it will be important to acquire and share knowledge; communication will be a key issue, as well as curiosity.

JUPITER IN CANCER
People born with Jupiter in Cancer stand out for relating to the world in a sensitive and compassionate way, with values centered on tradition.

JUPITER IN LEO
For people with Jupiter in Leo, personal recognition is essential. They'll have confident beliefs that they'll express with great force, but they tend to depend on the opinion of others.

JUPITER IN VIRGO
For people with Jupiter in Virgo, in addition to being detailed, analytical, and meticulous, they find it important to serve others, be useful, and contribute to the collective well-being.

JUPITER IN LIBRA
People with Jupiter in Libra seek harmony and justice, and their efforts will be through reform and by exhibiting sensitivity. This sensitivity can lead them to be indecisive and not create real processes.

JUPITER IN SCORPIO
People with Jupiter in Scorpio seek relationships through deep change and transformation. They're interested in the occult and the taboo. They will undergo a vital, profound transformation.

JUPITER IN SAGITTARIUS
For people with Jupiter in Sagittarius, expansion, exchange of ideas, cultural exchange, and physical, philosophical, and cerebral travel will shape their social identity.

JUPITER IN CAPRICORN
For people with Jupiter in Capricorn, their position in society, status, and success is important. They'll be constant researchers who strive to train until they achieve a well-defined identity of their own.

JUPITER IN AQUARIUS
People with Jupiter in Aquarius will have a revolutionary character; they will mark a milestone in their generation. They need to distinguish themselves from others, but in a role that benefits the majority. Tolerance will be key.

JUPITER IN PISCES
People with Jupiter in Pisces are characterized by a social sensitivity and empathy that can lead them to get involved in social and humanitarian processes. In addition, they have a personal and idealistic view of the world.

Saturn

Saturn is one of the first gods, connected to the passage of time. He's the father of Zeus and other important gods. The planet Saturn, like Jupiter, is a social planet. It governs responsibility, perseverance, and maturity. Since it takes nearly thirty years to travel its orbit, the time in life when Saturn returns to its position when we were born is known as the "return of Saturn." It's a point of introspection and goal setting for the next few years, as well as a moment to see where we're at that point.

Retrograde: 3 times a year
Changes sign every: 2½ years, approximately
Completes its orbit in: 29½ years

Ruler: Capricorn and Aquarius
Exaltation: Libra
Detriment: Cancer and Leo
Fall: Aries

Saturn in Each Sign

SATURN IN ARIES
People with Saturn in Aries may tend to mature late. They must learn to develop patience and responsibility, and they may have difficulty following orders.

SATURN IN TAURUS
Unlike Saturn in Aries, those with Saturn in Taurus tend to be conservative, mature from an early age, somewhat materialistic, and thrifty. They may hoard resources and possessions and be somewhat greedy.

SATURN IN GEMINI
People with Saturn in Gemini will highly value the right to express what they think; their fears will be related to having to hold back or not being able to express themselves freely.

SATURN IN CANCER

People with Saturn in Cancer tend to be more introspective and emotional. They may suffer from shyness or not being able to express what they feel.

SATURN IN LEO

People with Saturn in Leo, despite being sociable, may suffer self-esteem issues if they fail to create an impact or be of real relevance in their field of work or in society.

SATURN IN VIRGO

The person with Saturn in Virgo will be characterized as having a need for control over everything that surrounds them; if they aren't satisfied, they may be too controlling or a perfectionist, getting lost in the details.

SATURN IN LIBRA

The person with Saturn in Libra will seek the collective more than individualism. They'll be considerate, but indecision can lead them to not fulfill their objectives and feel dissatisfied. They'll seek relevance.

SATURN IN SCORPIO

The person with this position in Scorpio will generally have problems with attachments, both materially and emotionally. They will feel insecure and tend to be greedy.

SATURN IN SAGITTARIUS

The person with Saturn in Sagittarius needs to get out of their comfort zone—if they don't achieve fulfillment in this sense, they tend to feel imprisoned and stuck in routine and obligations.

SATURN IN CAPRICORN

People with Saturn in Capricorn are so ambitious that they can become excessive and ruthless in order to achieve success.

SATURN IN AQUARIUS

People with Saturn in Aquarius can feel different and like an outsider, and that can cause a fear of feeling excluded or alone.

SATURN IN PISCES

For people with Saturn in Pisces, the greatest risk is putting others before themselves; they can also be insecure and fearful. Loneliness scares them, as does not feeling loved.

Uranus

Uranus in mythology was one of the primordial Titans. He personified the sky and was the husband of Gaea. In astrology, Uranus is considered one of the transpersonal or generational planets. It governs everything related to rebellion, innovation, scientific and cultural advances, originality, and breaking with the old or traditional. The house of Uranus in our chart reveals in which sector of our life we will be more creative or rebellious. The planets that form aspects with Uranus will give a rebellious bonus to that factor of our personality.

Ruler: Aquarius
Exaltation: Scorpio
Detriment: Leo
Fall: Taurus

When Uranus retrogrades, we may feel the need to examine where we are stuck, how we can contribute effectively to the common good . . . It will last about four months, so we have time to review and, once it goes direct, change attitudes that no longer serve us.

Uranus in Each Sign

URANUS IN ARIES
Those with Uranus in Aries are risky people. They are eager to go on adventures, welcome change, and are enthusiastic by nature. They may engage in events in a hasty and thoughtless way.

URANUS IN TAURUS
Uranus in Taurus is a position that explores how to look for material, economic resources. Innovation is needed to find economic stability and tranquility.

URANUS IN GEMINI
Uranus in Gemini exemplifies a great desire to investigate and find innovative yet focused ways to open many possible windows; it doesn't delve into a single topic, it opens many new avenues.

URANUS IN CANCER

Uranus in Cancer explores an imbalance in our inner world, in our emotions, which invites us to reinvent ourselves and find emotional balance in a different way than what we are used to.

URANUS IN LEO

Uranus in Leo involves a genuine search (perhaps also somewhat selfish) for ourselves. People with Uranus in Leo want to be free and authentically themselves.

URANUS IN VIRGO

Uranus in Virgo explores innovation at work and research both in new areas of knowledge and in methods to be more effective and productive at work.

URANUS IN LIBRA

Uranus in Libra covers two fundamental issues: on the one hand, sentimental independence and the search for balance alone; on the other, innovation in law and justice.

URANUS IN SCORPIO

Uranus in Scorpio explores deep and transformative mental and emotional changes: drastic changes in religion, dogmas, or spirituality.

URANUS IN SAGITTARIUS

Uranus in Sagittarius explores the breaching of borders, new philosophies, and the openness of ideas. It features rejection of the closed and old and the need for freedom, through which a profound transformation will be achieved.

URANUS IN CAPRICORN

With Uranus in Capricorn, power structures and social and economic norms will be questioned. Power struggles, as well as social and professional changes, are key issues with this position.

URANUS IN AQUARIUS

Aquarius is in its domicile in Uranus. Idealism and group actions will benefit, and individual efforts will falter more. Progressive and open-minded, these people look to the future.

URANUS IN PISCES

With Uranus in Pisces, in the creative impulse and the subconscious, the seed of change will be born. Intuitively, ideas will emerge without materializing. Everything artistic and spiritual will be favored.

Neptune

Neptune in Roman mythology was the god of the seas; the Greek equivalent would be Poseidon. Neptune governs everything related to the subconscious, the intuitive, the artistic, and the dreamlike. He's also related to empathy, spiritual union, and, to some extent, the avoidance of reality. (This can also lead to drugs or substance abuse.) Neptune spends approximately fifteen years in each sign of the Zodiac, so it affects an entire generation. The house of Neptune tells us in which areas we can find ourselves confused and the aspects with Neptune give us greater insight into the areas that these planets dominate.

Ruler: Pisces
Exaltation: Cancer
Detriment: Virgo
Fall: Capricorn

Neptune in Each Sign

NEPTUNE IN ARIES
The creativity and imagination of Aries are governed by impulses, by sudden bursts of inspiration. If the confrontation between their reality and imagination is violent, they will strongly resist.

NEPTUNE IN TAURUS
Inspiration and ideals are found in everyday life, routine, and security with Neptune in Taurus. It features a powerful sense of intuition with others and intuition focused on material needs.

NEPTUNE IN GEMINI
Neptune in Gemini manifests as an intellectualized intuition; creativity appears open and the person is willing to communicate and cooperate.

NEPTUNE IN CANCER

With Neptune in Cancer, an extreme sensitivity is manifested but one that intuitively seeks security and the home. These people are prolific in artistic realms and fearful when it comes to facing harsh reality.

NEPTUNE IN LEO

Neptune in Leo is a position that favors an active, focused intuition that seeks open, creative impulse and its effect on other people. It favors the materialization of ideas.

NEPTUNE IN VIRGO

With Neptune in Virgo, a certain opposition to dreams, inspiration, and the artistic can be found, due to a need to rationalize and classify emotions.

NEPTUNE IN LIBRA

With Neptune in Libra, the maximum expression of the artistic, understood as symmetry and beauty, materializes. Idealism is embodied with justice, balance, and harmony.

NEPTUNE IN SCORPIO

Neptune in Scorpio delves into the human psyche. Creativity manifests as messy and chaotic, intense but with great capacity to explore fundamental truths of existence.

NEPTUNE IN SAGITTARIUS

With Neptune in Sagittarius, the interest lies in spiritual exploration, the search for answers, but in a much more chill and hippie sense than Scorpio. Inspiration is found in the world.

NEPTUNE IN CAPRICORN

These people hold many creative skills, but they're focused on and directed to obtain an objective, whether that be economic prosperity, social success, or productivity in some field.

NEPTUNE IN AQUARIUS

Neptune in Aquarius focuses creativity in an individualistic way, but with the intention of having an impact on society or a group. Artistic and spiritual innovation are strong themes.

NEPTUNE IN PISCES

Although Pisces is exalted in Neptune, so much ambiguity and confusion reinforce the creative character, but they weaken the intention of materialization. There's danger of idealization and distancing from reality.

Pluto

Pluto in Roman mythology is the god of the underworld; its Greek equivalent is Hades. The planet Pluto explores our deepest issues: life, death, transformation, liberation, closing cycles, anguish, sex and taboos, the forbidden, and what scares us at a deeper level. The house in which Pluto is found will tell us in which area we are most afraid of change. Aspects with Pluto will challenge the person to integrate issues into their life that may be initially difficult.

Ruler: Scorpio
Exaltation: Pisces
Detriment: Taurus
Fall: Virgo

Pluto in Each Sign

PLUTO IN ARIES
With Pluto in Aries, the desire for change will manifest itself impulsively, viscerally, radically, and even thoughtlessly and violently, but there may be lack of determination to finish what was started.

PLUTO IN TAURUS
With Pluto in the stable sign Taurus, there will be a fear of losing this stability, materially and financially as well as emotionally, and some difficulty in adapting to change.

PLUTO IN GEMINI
With Pluto in Gemini, the person will have an intense need to express themselves, and share with others everything they are. Common are a great need for openness, problems with introspection, or periods of loneliness.

PLUTO IN CANCER

With Pluto in Cancer, a dichotomy arises: on the one hand, there's a strong connection with what they know (people, family, their mother); on the other, all these familiar aspects will be a reason for confrontation.

PLUTO IN LEO

Pluto in Leo gives individuals a strong capacity for attraction, personal magnetism, charisma, and a desire to fight, but they have an individualism and fierce competitiveness that can work against them.

PLUTO IN VIRGO

With Pluto in Virgo, the obsession with details may be such that they lose perspective on things and on the bigger picture. There can be deep transformations in the workplace.

PLUTO IN LIBRA

Pluto in Libra produces a desire for perfection that can lead to trying to change people or situations instead of accepting them and moving on, which can cause a great imbalance.

PLUTO IN SCORPIO

With Pluto in Scorpio, the transformations will be painful, deep, and necessary. From death a new life will arise, like the phoenix. These people are skilled investigators of prohibited subjects.

PLUTO IN SAGITTARIUS

With Pluto in Sagittarius, the fundamental need will be to discover and learn about new ideas, values, and beliefs, oftentimes seeking them abroad. This search will be essential for their development.

PLUTO IN CAPRICORN

The determination to improve and achieve goals, as well as to embrace materialism (in its most positive but also negative aspects), will characterize the natives of Pluto in Capricorn.

PLUTO IN AQUARIUS

Through rebellion and originality, those born with Pluto in Aquarius will tear down the most archaic, rigid, and conventional structures. They participate in great revolutions and social struggles.

PLUTO IN PISCES

Pluto in Pisces produces individuals who are deeply connected with magic and mysticism. These people have a great empathy, dreaminess, and idealism.

The Ascendant
(and the Descendent)

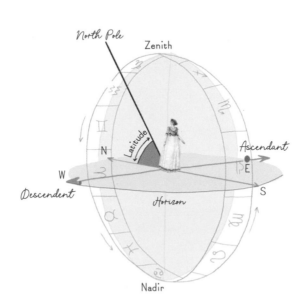

North Pole

Zenith

Latitude

N

W

Descendent

Horizon

Nadir

Ascendant

E

S

The ascendant, together with the Sun and the Moon, is the most important position in our birth chart. It's a geometric point (shown on the drawing above): the ascendant is the intersection between the horizon line and the Zodiac wheel. The sign where the ascendant is found changes in a matter of minutes; that's why knowing the exact time of the person's birth is crucial in identifying it. While the Sun describes the energy we have at birth and the Moon explores our inner world, the ascendant is the energy within us that we must unearth throughout our lives, through the experiences we live and the people we meet. It also plays a fundamental role in how others perceive us. For example, have you ever been told that you're very sweet but you believe yourself to have a strong personality? It may be that your Sun or Mars is in a fire sign (remember that the Sun speaks of basic energy, and Mars, among other things, of impulse and violence) and you have an ascendant in water that makes you seem sweeter and shier than you really are. It's also common to feel attracted to people who have the Sun in your ascendant's sign: the energy that attracts you is already within you, but since you still don't know quite how to manifest it (which is typical of the ascendant), you're attracted to people who possess it naturally. Let's explore what traits the ascendant gives each sign. The descendent is the opposite point, the opposite sign, and it describes the energy that we will need to assimilate and learn throughout our life to fully develop.

The Ascendant in Each Sign

The Aries ascendant speaks of sociable people with a temper, who are somewhat impatient and nervous. The Libra descendant shows that this person will need to learn to be more balanced and seek harmony in their relationships.

The Taurus ascendant describes a person who appears calm and docile, surely much more than what they feel inside. This person is affectionate. The Scorpio descendant teaches them to learn to let go and forgive.

The Gemini ascendant speaks of a restless and somewhat scattered person. They enjoy good conversations. The Sagittarius descendant shows that they should seek the meaning of things.

The Cancer ascendant makes the person appear affectionate but reserved, and sensitive but irritable. The Capricorn descendant indicates that they need to be more rational and pragmatic.

The Leo ascendant describes an outspoken, charismatic person, although they don't perceive themselves as such. The Aquarius descendent shows them the importance of focusing on the collective.

The Virgo ascendant makes the person appear reserved, organized, and calm. The Pisces descendent shows them the value of sensitivity, emotions, and empathy.

The Libra ascendant makes the person seek harmony in their relationships and in their environment. The Aries descendant shows them the value of fearlessly expressing their opinion and their limits.

The Scorpio ascendant makes the person seem somewhat mysterious. The Taurus descendant shows them the need to reconcile themselves with uncertainty, to avoid falling into materialism and utilitarianism in their relationships.

The Sagittarius ascendant speaks of people attracted to adventure, who appear carefree and even somewhat chaotic. The Gemini descendant encourages its natives to avoid falling into zealotry and to cultivate tolerance.

The Capricorn ascendant seems more serious and disciplined than they are—they're attracted to formal, traditional people. The Cancer descendant invites them to get in touch with their sensitive side and to prioritize the home.

The Aquarius ascendant makes a person seem eccentric, and they're attracted to individuals with these qualities. The Leo descendant demands that these natives set aside self-centeredness and balance the personal and the social.

The Pisces ascendant will make the person sweet, somewhat shy, and clueless. They're sensitive to the energy around them. The Virgo descendant will need order, discipline, and guidelines to fully develop their potential.

The Midheaven

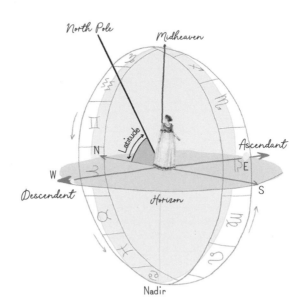

The midheaven is the highest point of our birth chart, as seen in the drawing on this page, and it's related to the tenth house (your midheaven sign is the one that was in that house at the time of your birth). The midheaven informs us about our potential and aspirations, which we can develop according to our circumstances and level of consciousness. In other words, the midheaven tells us which path to follow to develop ourselves to the fullest and meet our goals, especially at a professional level. It's not that the midheaven says, "Look, Mary, you have to be an engineer," but rather it gives us an idea of what areas show promise or what approaches we can use to focus on them. The information that the midheaven provides may also refer to a more spiritual sense or our general approach to life (like the need to go abroad, participate in cultural exchanges, or focus more on creating a home or establishing ourselves in a familiar place). The midheaven's vocation will have to be developed in common; in other words, in society and in concert with others. The aspects with the midheaven can favor, accelerate, delay, or hinder this development, depending on whether they're positive or more limiting. You'll learn about the aspects in "The Birth Chart" (page 152), after exploring what each house means; then you'll learn how the birth chart is interpreted. If your Sun and your midheaven coincide, you will have no problem finding your purpose, it will happen naturally.

The Midheaven in Each Sign

The midheaven in Aries speaks of positions of leadership, entrepreneurship, love of risk, and adventure. It signifies the path of the leader who creates a new way. Pay attention to sports and physical activity.

The midheaven in Taurus speaks of the relationship with the earth, tradition, crafts, heritage preservation, and sensitivity to people, especially the elderly and children.

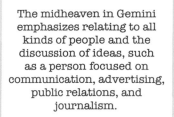

The midheaven in Gemini emphasizes relating to all kinds of people and the discussion of ideas, such as a person focused on communication, advertising, public relations, and journalism.

The midheaven in Cancer speaks of the vocation to help others in an empathetic way. It suggests a relationship with medicine, psychology, or generally helping the most disadvantaged as well as friends and family.

The midheaven in Leo speaks of entrepreneurship and leadership but is more focused on politics or issues that have to do with charisma rather than work or risk.

The midheaven in Virgo describes a person who usually finds a specific topic that they're passionate about and dedicates their efforts to becoming an expert in that area.

The midheaven in Libra speaks of the purpose of finding balance, justice, harmony, and equality, especially in relationships, but it can also be related to professions in the legal field (judges, lawyers, and so on).

The midheaven in Scorpio speaks of tireless and even obsessive researchers, whose purpose will be to master some art or investigative area. Psychiatry, history, archaeology, esotericism, or religion are relevant topics.

The midheaven in Sagittarius describes a person's need to leave their place of origin and see the world, research foreign philosophies, marry a foreigner, or simply open up to people in general.

The midheaven in Capricorn is undoubtedly related to careers, or at least to the organization and management of resources. Problem-solving and general financial matters have to do with this midheaven.

The midheaven in Aquarius describes innovative people, unique or eccentric. They would undoubtedly be excellent teachers who spark their students' interest.

The midheaven in Pisces describes people focused on the artistic and psychological. Their fundamental concern will be to investigate the sensitive and occult, always seeking the spiritual and dealing with their own and others' emotional issues.

Chiron and Other Celestial Bodies

In Greek mythology, Chiron was a cultured, considerate, and elegant centaur, unlike the other centaurs who were ignorant and insensitive. The planetoid Chiron was discovered in 1977, making it a very recent addition to astrology. Both Chiron and the asteroids Ceres, Pallas, Vesta, and Juno describe partial qualities that color the meaning and implications of the rest of the planets and aspects.

Chiron: Points to everything that causes us insecurities or pain. It represents where our spiritual wounds are and where we should focus our healing efforts to help others and especially ourselves.

Ceres: Goddess of agriculture, in astrology she represents short processes, the day-to-day, and how we manage resources.

Pallas: Pallas Athena was the Greek goddess of strategy, chastity, and reason. In astrology, she represents creative ability and problem-solving.

Vesta: Goddess of the home, she is related to sexual creativity and the homey feeling in relationships.

Juno: Roman goddess of marriage, she is associated with commitment, jealousy, and loyalty.

✽ Chiron in Each Sign ✽

Insecurity. Fear of taking the initiative. Physical complexes.

Fear of not having money or resources. Doubt about their own abilities.

Fear of not being understood and not trusting their own ideas.

Fear of not belonging and not feeling loved and valued.

Fear of ridicule, of looking weird, or of not having friends.

Tendency to organize other people's affairs and neglect their own.

Fear of commitment, closeness, and getting hurt.

Fear of abandonment or loss, loneliness. They feel different.

Existential dilemmas and fear of not finding meaning in life.

Social and economic dissatisfaction.

Easily carried away by others due to lack of their own judgment.

Insecurity and fear of abandonment. Emotional dependence.

✻ Ceres in Each Sign ✻

Independent, decisive, and autonomous.

Needs to protect, care for, and pamper others.

Cultivates the mind by reading; learning is essential.

Needs to receive and give love. Insecure.

High self-esteem and motivates others.

Neat, orderly, and efficient.

Good group coordinator and organizer.

Invites others to dig deeper and investigate.

Teaches people to open up and learn from others.

Provides security and confidence.

Teaches others to love without toxic attachments.

Relieves emotional distress and is supportive.

✻ Pallas in Each Sign ✻

Impulsive, fast, and efficient but reckless.

Patient, seeks long-term solutions, and calm.

Versatile and helps others to solve problems on their own.

Focuses on family comfort and emotional support.

Feels the need to lead and be obeyed.

Focuses on detailed strategies.

Seeks fair and impartial solutions.

Skilled in solving mysteries and discovering the occult.

Seeks to delve into the philosophical and share that knowledge.

Perseveres and is disciplined until they find the best way out.

Seeks utopian and experimental solutions.

Develops intuitive solutions to subjective problems.

✽ Juno in Each Sign ✽

Seeks an energetic partner with character and determination.

Seeks someone who provides warmth and stability.

Attracted to restless minds and intelligence.

Appreciates traditional values and stability.

Seeks a passionate partner who will adore them.

Desires a stable and reliable partner.

Seeks someone balanced, harmonious, and beautiful.

Seeks someone with emotional depth and intensity.

Seeks someone optimistic, cheerful, and adventurous.

Looks for someone who gives them stability.

Their ideal partner is independent and original.

Their ideal partner is sensitive and idealistic.

✽ Vesta in Each Sign ✽

Dynamic and contrary to routine.

Continuous and stable efforts.

Quick ideas, brainstorming, and multitasking.

Cuddly and emotional processes.

Good at leading groups and being alone.

Meticulous and rigorous processes.

Seeks perfection in beauty and harmony.

Intimate, deep, and radical work.

Philosophical search for the truth. Uncompromising.

Commitment, dedication, insistence, and ambition.

Free and creative process. Somewhat chaotic.

Intuitive, fanciful, and imaginative.

5. The Houses

The houses in astrology are the areas of life where the planets intervene. To make them easy to understand, let's explore them as twelve segments of the circumference. The first house is located in the same spot as the ascendant, and the rest of the houses depart from this position. Let's check out what each house means, and in the next chapter (page 152) we will finally join all the concepts we have discussed (signs, houses, planets, and so forth) to understand our birth chart and how some things are related to others.

For now, let's explore what issues are represented in each house. We'll start with the first house, which has to do with our sense of identity, and we'll continue ascending until we reach the most spiritual one, the twelfth house, passing through our place in society, friendships, romantic relationships, and more. Let's go!

The First House

The first house is related to the sign of Aries and the ascendant. The first house describes our sense of identity, self-image, and first impression.

The ascendant is always in the first house; from there the houses are distributed in ascending order. If you have a planet in the first house, it will have a great role in your personality: it will be very present.

Sun in the first house: Very positive position, gives security and charisma to the native of this position. Luck accompanies them.

Moon in the first house: This person's emotional world will be rich and will have a strong impact on their life. This position can give a certain shyness or introversion to their character.

Mercury in the first house: The intellectual plane is prominent.

Venus in the first house: These attractive people find it important to be liked and to play the game of love.

Mars in the first house: It gives the person great determination; they can be seen as single-minded and even belligerent.

Saturn in the first house: This position makes the person need to be recognized by society. In social relationships, they can easily feel excluded and self-conscious.

Jupiter in the first house: This person stands out among others.

Uranus in the first house: This different, innovative, and peculiar person is destined to make a novel impact on society.

Neptune in the first house: This results in a person with great sensitivity to the spiritual or subconscious.

Pluto in the first house: This person will face important challenges in life but will emerge victorious from them; they have the ability to endlessly reinvent themselves.

The Second House

The second house is related to the sign of Taurus. This house tells us about our resources to achieve our objectives and goals, both materially and intellectually or socially. It also refers to how we manage those resources and whether we're organized, scattered, or lazy, which will depend on the planets inhabiting the house and what sign it is in. A chart with multiple placements in the second house will indicate a person who's quite attached to the material.

Sun in the second house: To feel fulfilled, this person needs to reach a certain level of financial and material stability, and to learn to organize themselves well.

Moon in the second house: Emotional security is provided by a certain level of financial stability.

Mercury in the second house: These people have a practical and business-oriented approach.

Venus in the second house: This offers good luck in money and material resources.

Mars in the second house: This can signify greedy or object-focused, impatient, and materialistic people.

Saturn in the second house: This is associated with someone who is stingy and somewhat obsessed with not running out of money.

Jupiter in the second house: It's a very good position for material success; it will be easy for them to get rich or earn a lot of money.

Uranus in the second house: It can indicate possible economic crises throughout their lives; it will be difficult for these people to achieve stability.

Neptune in the second house: This signifies people detached from the material. They enjoy sharing.

Pluto in the second house: These people can tend to hoard belongings because it makes them feel secure.

The Third House

The third house is associated with Gemini. It represents our way of communicating with the people closest to us: siblings, close friends, or neighbors. It's also associated with our way of forming superficial relationships, our ability to make friends, and the types of things that spark our curiosity and interests. A very powerful third house (one with many planets in it) will indicate people whose close networks will be important to them.

Sun in the third house: For this person, it will be essential to seek their sense of self through knowledge, reading, and intellectualism.

Moon in the third house: It will be easy for these people to communicate their emotions and for others to show them how they feel.

Mercury in the third house: The third house belongs to Gemini, which is ruled by Mercury; it's a good position. Communication and learning will be easy for these natives.

Venus in the third house: Relating to others comes easy, especially on an intellectual level. Mental stimulation will be essential to establish a romantic relationship.

Mars in the third house: Reasoning will be these natives' most powerful weapon.

Saturn in the third house: These people have a fear of being misunderstood and not being able to express what they feel.

Jupiter in the third house: Communication will be a strong point in their work life.

Uranus in the third house: This signifies innovative, original individuals with great creativity.

Neptune in the third house: This house influences creativity in a spiritual, dreamlike, and sensitive sense.

Pluto in the third house: Discovering the hidden and mysterious, as well as fraternal relationships, will have great importance for these people.

The Fourth House

The fourth house belongs to Cancer. Generally speaking, it represents connection with family, with tradition and values. In our adulthood, this house will be reflected in our choice of partner, since the fourth house gives us an idea of what type of relationships make us feel comfortable and safe, and of our concept of intimacy inherited from our family. A powerful fourth house (one with many planets in it) speaks of the crucial importance of family.

Sun in the fourth house: These people recognize the importance of family when it comes to discovering their purpose; it can be in the sense of their family heritage, values, or ancestors, or the family that they create.

Moon in the fourth house: This person will find their refuge in the known, in traditions, and in the familiar, both in a literal and more spiritual sense.

Mercury in the fourth house: This person is more likely to have conservative values. Tradition is important to develop mentally.

Venus in the fourth house: This person tends to be affectionate in a familiar sense and tries to be a figure of trust and care.

Mars in the fourth house: Their goal when faced with a conflict is to protect themselves and their loved ones.

Saturn in the fourth house: This indicates possible conflicts with family relationships; they need to create a life outside the family unit.

Jupiter in the fourth house: A very good house for Jupiter: people tend to feel integrated into their family and will attach great importance to these ties.

Uranus in the fourth house: They may feel somewhat alienated or distant from their family, as if they're outcasts or don't quite fit in.

Neptune in the fourth house: The longing for childhood or that feeling that "everything was better in the past" can consume these people.

Pluto in the fourth house: They're often interested in genealogy or family inheritance, as well as airing dirty laundry.

The Fifth House

The fifth house is the one linked to Leo. It represents how we like to stand out. It also describes which people we are attracted to, as well as how we interact with others romantically. It also speaks of innocence, our inner world, how we like to feel valued, and in what ways we show appreciation. A powerful fifth house (one with many planets in it) represents an attractive person or someone who finds it important to be liked, sensually speaking.

Sun in the fifth house: A good house for the Sun; it will give these people charisma and success.

Moon in the fifth house: Somewhat dependent on the approval of others, especially in youth, people in this position will tend to live on the outside, neglecting their emotional world.

Mercury in the fifth house: Great public speaking skills, charisma, and passion when presenting ideas are characteristics of this position.

Venus in the fifth house: These people tend to look for romantic partners who offer them plenty of attention, and they can remain in that physical superficiality if they aren't well aspected.

Mars in the fifth house: These people will be emphatic, passionate, and even fierce in an argument. It's a powerful position.

Saturn in the fifth house: Their biggest fears can be related to not feeling recognized and realizing that they're not relevant to others.

Jupiter in the fifth house: This is a very favorable position to feel fulfilled in general and to obtain professional recognition without excessive effort.

Uranus in the fifth house: It's a somewhat complicated position. People here tend to feel trapped and somewhat dissatisfied with their life.

Neptune in the fifth house: They may find it difficult to reconcile reality with their fantasies and wishes, and may feel somewhat confused in this regard.

Pluto in the fifth house: With a tendency to mix the forbidden with the ardent, they will experience important passions throughout their lives.

The sixth house is the one linked to Virgo. It's associated with two aspects: on the one hand, subordinate relationships (bosses, employees, and hierarchy); on the other, routine, daily work, perseverance, health, and their way of organizing study and work times. The planets in this house also represent the habits that affect health.

Sun in the sixth house: This will be a person who can live a full life, but if the position is not well aspected, they can tend to be monotonous or lack significant ambitions.

Moon in the sixth house: They find safety and feel at home in routines, the little things in life, order, and an existence without major upheavals.

Mercury in the sixth house: They tend to focus on the objective. Organization and written communication can be their forte.

Venus in the sixth house: In their emotional bonds, they'll look for love daily; turbulent passions can destabilize them.

Mars in the sixth house: Very focused on daily work, they value effort and dedication.

Saturn in the sixth house: This position tends to fear loss of stability and the unforeseen events of life.

Jupiter in the sixth house: These people have a great spirit of sacrifice and put in constant effort to achieve their goals.

Uranus in the sixth house: They can suffer from a lack of patience or perseverance both in their relationships and in the workplace.

Neptune in the sixth house: People in this position give themselves to others with a spirit of dedication and sacrifice.

Pluto in the sixth house: This position features great resilience and tenacity to get out of trouble.

The Seventh House

The seventh house is related to Libra and the descendant, and it represents our way of relating, collaborating, and making commitments. While the first house describes our sense of *self*, the seventh house deals with *us*. These relationships can be work related, sentimental, or legal. It can also represent our ability to maintain long-term relationships.

Sun in the seventh house: The chances of success are increased through contact with others. Friends who become partners are frequent.

Moon in the seventh house: The feeling of protection will be achieved through harmonious and balanced relationships, as well as an aesthetically balanced and pleasant environment.

Mercury in the seventh house: These people usually work so that all parties reach an agreement.

Venus in the seventh house: Romantic relationships will be favored by this position.

Mars in the seventh house: These people will advocate for justice first and foremost in a conflict.

Saturn in the seventh house: They'll tend to be a bit extreme in relationships with others.

Jupiter in the seventh house: These people have luck in finances and work, but always rely on a network of contacts that protects them.

Uranus in the seventh house: This influences the bonds with other people, making natives in this position surprising and unconventional.

Neptune in the seventh house: With a great capacity to forgive, heal, and deepen romantic relationships, these people provide balance to those who are by their side.

Pluto in the seventh house: A propensity for stormy and forbidden relationships can create upheaval in the person.

The Eighth House

The eighth house is related to Scorpio. This house is all about the occult, the mysterious, taboos, and deep analysis. All the planets in this house will acquire a Scorpio nuance: deep transformation processes in the issues that this planet regulates, great intuition, but also secrecy and mystery. It also has to do with the relationship we have with other people's resources (as opposed to the second house, our own resources).

Sun in the eighth house: The person who has this position will experience many challenges. Interests related to spirituality and even death.

Moon in the eighth house: They need to establish a lot of intimacy with people and have a great transforming energy. Possible conflicts exist with parents, especially the mother.

Mercury in the eighth house: They tend to lose information and suffer frequent misunderstandings, but they also have a great ability to research and delve deep into things.

Venus in the eighth house: Possible conflicts arise due to jealousy, possessiveness, and drama. They need to merge with their loved ones.

Mars in the eighth house: They handle themselves with sharpness and great dexterity; they are thrifty and persistent.

Saturn in the eighth house: It favors that, in old age, the person will enjoy a kind of spiritual calm, and it will be a beautiful stage in their life.

Jupiter in the eighth house: This defines a predisposition to receive money from sources other than work: inheritances and marriages, for example. Also signifies an ability to save and manage money.

Uranus in the eighth house: It features interest in the paranormal.

Neptune in the eighth house: A spirituality focused on the border between dreams and reality, life and death, is found in this position.

Pluto in the eighth house: They will undergo transformations of intimate and spiritual depth.

The Ninth House

The ninth house is related to Sagittarius. In general, this house pertains to what is far away. It may be associated with travel, foreign philosophies, relationships with people from other countries, and the search for the meaning of life. It's opposite the third house (belonging to Gemini, representing relationships with what is nearby; see page 142). If this house is powerful in the chart, the search for wisdom and knowledge will be one of the engines that drive that person's life.

Sun in the ninth house: This person is predisposed to travel or to create their life in a place other than where they were born, as well as interested in faraway lands and cultures.

Moon in the ninth house: This signals the need for expansion and freedom, but also for spiritual search.

Mercury in the ninth house: The person seeks learning on the philosophical and spiritual planes, and holds an interest in foreign philosophies.

Venus in the ninth house: It's likely the people with whom they establish a closer spiritual connection will be foreigners or won't live in the same place as this person.

Mars in the ninth house: This position marks the impulse to expand both physical and spiritual horizons.

Saturn in the ninth house: With this Saturn, there are frequent crises of faith and the search—often unsatisfactory—for a greater explanation that gives meaning to life.

Jupiter in the ninth house: Wealth is understood as spiritual wealth.

Uranus in the ninth house: This idealistic person will dream of traveling and stunning experiences.

Neptune in the ninth house: This person will seek to create and live in an ideal world that is sometimes perceived as impossible.

Pluto in the ninth house: Deep spiritual search, different religious beliefs, spiritual tendencies, and travel—this person will create their own creed.

The Tenth House

The tenth house is related to the midheaven and the sign of Capricorn. This house represents our level of satisfaction, our ability to achieve goals, and the part we play in society. The planets that occupy this house show us the way to persevere, achieve our goals, and feel satisfied in life.

Sun in the tenth house: This ambitious person aspires to obtain wealth and improve their social position. Given this disposition, they can relegate other aspects of their life if they're not well aspected.

Moon in the tenth house: They need status and wealth to feel emotionally secure.

Mercury in the tenth house: This person has very clear objectives and an alert and organized mind.

Venus in the tenth house: These are people who, when starting a relationship, take into account their status and what that person can provide rationally; they are less prone to romanticism.

Mars in the tenth house: Being focused on ambition and the social ladder, reasoning, and objectivity are their main traits.

Saturn in the tenth house: Fear of losing their reputation, being ridiculed, or suffering financial loss are characteristics of this position.

Jupiter in the tenth house: This is a very good house for Jupiter. Its people tend to thrive financially and move up the social ladder.

Uranus in the tenth house: This position gives a lot of character and charisma and signals natural leaders who want to transform society or establish a new status quo.

Neptune in the tenth house: This person's lifestyle will be sophisticated but also somewhat bohemian and with a tendency to appreciate art in all its forms. They can tend toward snobbery.

Pluto in the tenth house: Dominant and ambitious people with natural charisma, they tend to push moral boundaries to access positions of power.

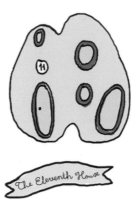

The Eleventh House

The eleventh house is related to the sign of Aquarius. It represents our place in society, how to feel integrated in a group, our sense of belonging to something bigger, more transcendental, and more influential than ourselves. It describes our place of influence in a group—but in social groups, not in our closest environment. Those with a powerful eleventh house will be influential people who, through their ability to innovate, will make an impact.

Sun in the eleventh house: This Sun is characterized by shining in groups, among friends, and in society.

Moon in the eleventh house: This position signals emotional need for expansion with others.

Mercury in the eleventh house: Communicative, innovative, and artistic people are found here.

Venus in the eleventh house: These people are independent but also need intellectual stimulation in a relationship.

Mars in the eleventh house: They express themselves in a personal and original way, yet create an impact in the group.

Saturn in the eleventh house: With difficulty feeling part of a group, they tend toward isolation.

Jupiter in the eleventh house: Relationships with powerful people will guarantee their success.

Uranus in the eleventh house: They're original, special, and different, and they don't go unnoticed.

Neptune in the eleventh house: This person will seek to relate to special people, because they also consider themselves as such.

Pluto in the eleventh house: It's difficult for them to adapt to reality. Emotional failures are possible.

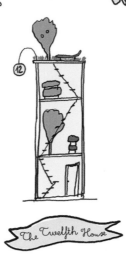

The Twelfth House

The twelfth house is related to the sign of Pisces, and it's the most spiritual house of them all. This house closes the Zodiac wheel. It represents the mind, the psyche, the collective unconscious, and the mystical. Given its extreme sensitivity, it also informs us of fears and insecurities, problems setting limits, and everything related to sacrifice and spiritual union. The planet in this house will have very sensitive but insecure nuances in the area it influences.

Sun in the twelfth house: It may influence whether the person feels sad, melancholic, or lonely.

Moon in the twelfth house: These dreamy people usually create their emotional refuge in their inner world, suffering when it comes to giving themselves to others.

Mercury in the twelfth house: Communication can be confusing, but they have an ability to perceive the spiritual and abstract.

Venus in the twelfth house: They seek solitude and time for themselves. It's difficult for them to establish meaningful personal relationships—they're shy and somewhat withdrawn.

Mars in the twelfth house: Individualistic and independent people, yet they are sensitive and intuitive.

Saturn in the twelfth house: They balance between being independent and being in a group. The twelfth house's spirituality balances Saturn's fear.

Jupiter in the twelfth house: Jupiter protects from the psychic intensity of this house.

Uranus in the twelfth house: These people often feel misunderstood and isolated from their environment.

Neptune in the twelfth house: These are people with a prolific inner world who easily manifest themselves and have psychic or artistic abilities.

Pluto in the twelfth house: Pluto in this house is one of the deepest and most intuitive positions on a mental and subconscious level. It features a deep search of mysterious and taboo issues.

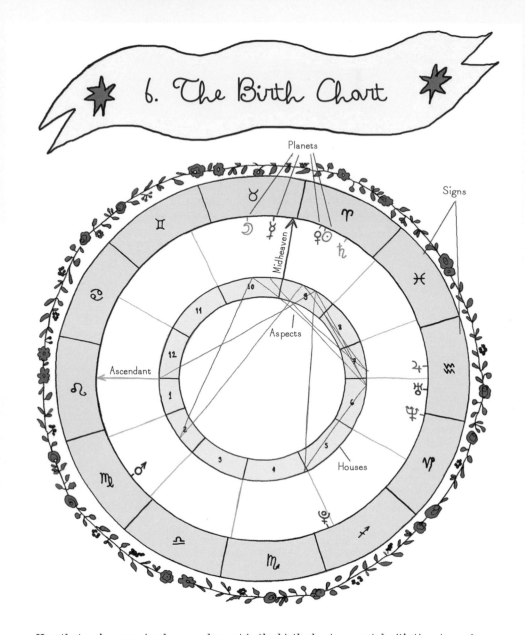

6. The Birth Chart

Planets

Signs

Midheaven

Aspects

Ascendant

Houses

Now that we've examined every element in the birth chart separately, it's time to explore how the birth chart is interpreted. The birth chart is the map that shows the position of each planet at the time and in the place each of us was born, and this describes the energy we had at birth. Let's recall what we've discussed so far, as seen in the illustration above:

Signs: They're in the outermost wheel, with the symbols of each sign.

Planets: The symbols represent the position of the planets with respect to the sign and the house (☽, ♂, ☿, and so on).

Houses: The area of life where astrology takes place, represented on the inner wheel with numbers (each number represents the house number).

And now we have a clearer picture of the aspects (represented by the lines that join some planets with others). As we'll see next, aspects show how the planets are related depending on whether the angles among them are favorable or unfavorable. To get your birth chart for the first time, you must enter the place, date, and time of your birth into an online calculator.

Aspects: Angles among Planets

The aspects are the angles that the planets form among each other. Some aspects are positive and harmonic; they create cooperation in matters that are influenced by these planets and tend to make the person feel satisfied in those areas. Other aspects are tense, and they make the person feel that these areas are a challenge to overcome. To measure aspects once the birth chart is drawn, use a protractor. The most important aspects are the following:

Conjunction ☌ 0°

This occurs when two or more planets are very close together (between 0 degrees and 10 degrees). It's also considered a conjunction if they're close in the same sign. This is a favorable aspect—the planets work together.

Stellium

This is a grouping of three or more planets in the same sign. It strengthens your energy. The more planets you have in a sign, the more of that sign you are: "You're such a Pisces!" "Of course, I have stellium in Pisces, girl."

Sextile ✳60°

The sextile is an aspect of approximately 60 degrees and is considered favorable. It connotes communication and harmony between the planets involved, meaning a little effort will go a long way.

Square □ 90°

This is a strong, unfavorable aspect where two planets form 90 degrees. The energies of the two planets will reveal a tension that the person must integrate and work on.

Trine △ 120°

The trine is an aspect between two planets that forms 120 degrees. It's powerful and benevolent, and the two planets will collaborate in harmony and peace. It can be very powerful.

Quincunx ⚻ 150°

The quincunx is an aspect between two planets that forms 150 degrees. Its effect unites, in a surprising and dynamic way, elements of life that are not generally communicated or related.

Opposition ☍ 180°

This is a 180-degree aspect that confronts two planets. It's a powerful aspect that will make the two planets fight, and it will be difficult for the person to assimilate. It creates fears and insecurities.

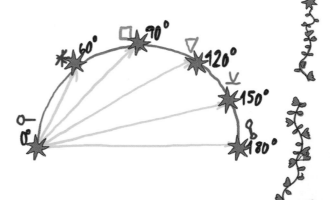

When a chart is highly concentrated in one of the four quadrants, it will have implications that are generally understood as follows:

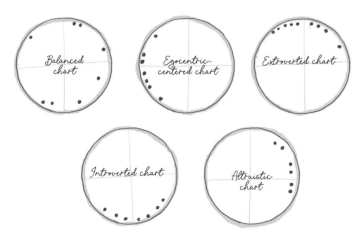

In addition to viewing the birth chart as a circle graph, you can read it as a list, or you can simply write down which sign and house the planet is located in to understand it more directly. Both the list and the graph provide the same information, although the graph is more complete, since the aspects and orientations are seen directly.

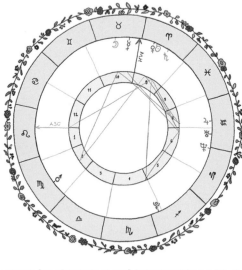

☉	Sun	Aries in the ninth house
☽	Moon	Taurus in the tenth house
☿	Mercury	Taurus in the tenth house
♀	Venus	Aries in the ninth house
♂	Mars	Virgo in the second house
♃	Jupiter	Aquarius in the seventh house
♄	Saturn	Aries in the ninth house
♅	Uranus	Aquarius in the sixth house
♆	Neptune	Capricorn in the sixth house
♇	Pluto	Sagittarius in the fourth house
☊	North Node	Libra in the eleventh house
☋	South Node	Aries in the eleventh house
ASC	Ascendant	Leo in the first house
MH	Midheaven	Taurus in the tenth house

Next, I leave you with basic instructions for obtaining and interpreting a birth chart. You'll also find a blank circle graph on which you can draw your own birth chart right in this book—or trace it and use it as a template.

To practice, do the following exercise with your own birth chart or with one belonging to a family member or friend.

1. Find an online birth chart calculator and enter the data (the person's name and the place, date, and time of birth).

2. On the template on the next page, enter the information: name, place, date, and time.

3. Draw the symbol of the ascendant sign and the first house, matching them one on top of the other, and distribute the rest of the signs and houses in Zodiac order around the birth chart graph.

4. Write down the signs and houses of all the planets.

5. Now it's time to place the planets. Keep in mind that each sign has 30 degrees, but to start learning, place the symbol of each planet in its sign (similar to the example on the previous page) close to its degree. If you aren't sure how to do it, use the online calculator as a reference, but reason through each planet's place.

6. Now that you can see which house and sign each planet is in, write them down in the lower-left list. Is there a sign where several planets are concentrated? Empty houses? Any house where several planets are concentrated? Jot it all down on the notes page (following the template) and write out what it means. It's okay if you don't remember everything! Consult the relevant pages in this book to see what each piece means.

7. Finally, we're missing only the aspects. To see them, you need a ruler and a protractor. Using a fine-point pencil, join the planet with the chart's center. The point where the line intersects with the circle of the houses is the one that you must join to see the aspects (see the example on the opposite page). Once this is done, determine if the planets form the indicated aspects (conjunction, sextile, opposition, and so forth). To find out what an aspect means:

   a. Analyze which planets are involved, then see what energy pertains to each of these issues and which house they're in.
   b. Explore the aspect's implications.
   c. Write down what kind of dynamics there will be between these planets.

8. Make a general assessment of the chart: Does it have a lot of energy in any element? Does it have multiple squares? Draw your own conclusions and practice with your friends to learn to detect patterns; it's a matter of trial and error and intuition.

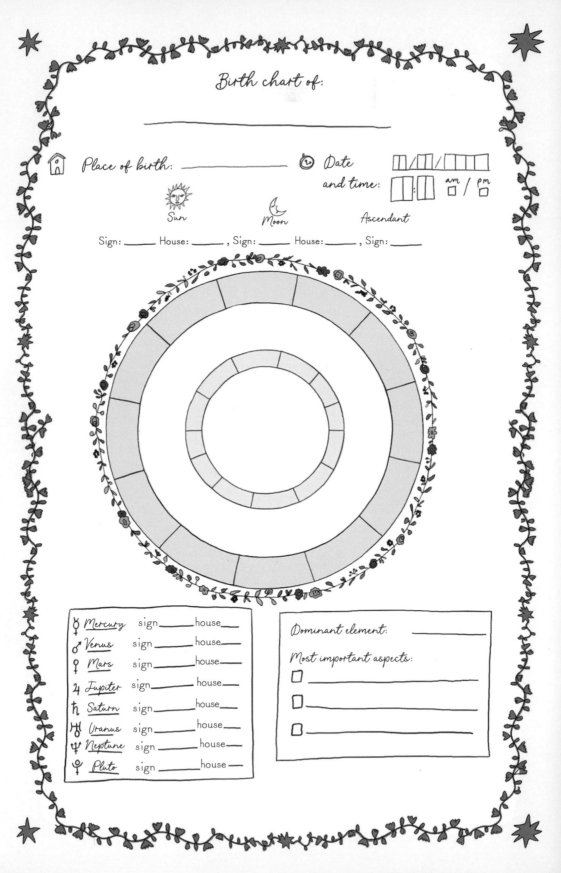

Birth chart of:

_____

🏠 Place of birth: _____   🕐 Date □/□/□□
                                        and time: □□:□□ am/pm

☀️ Sun   🌙 Moon   Ascendant

Sign: _____ House: _____ , Sign: _____ House: _____ , Sign: _____

☿ Mercury   sign_____ house___
♂ Venus   sign_____ house___
♀ Mars   sign_____ house___
♃ Jupiter   sign_____ house___
♄ Saturn   sign_____ house___
♅ Uranus   sign_____ house___
♆ Neptune   sign_____ house___
♇ Pluto   sign_____ house___

Dominant element: _____

Most important aspects:

☐ _____
☐ _____
☐ _____

Interpretation Notes

Frequently Asked AstroQuestions

What happens with twins?

As we briefly touched on early in this book (see page 18), the birth charts of twins are studied by complementary opposites. To understand the birth chart of twins in a simple way, calculate the birth chart normally. Write down the planets, houses, and signs in list form, and next to them write the complementary opposites of each position:

Twin 1   Twin 2
Sun: Taurus   Sun: Scorpio
Moon: Leo   Moon: Aquarius

and so on with the rest of the positions.

Which is which? To find out which birth chart belongs to each twin, simply analyze both, talk to them, and each person will immediately know which chart they most identify with. This complementary-energies thing between twins happens because their personalities, although they may seem different, are two sides of the same coin, which is why their paths in life rarely separate.

If I'm not compatible with my partner because of my Sun sign, what do I do? Do I leave them?

Of course not! Being "incompatible" in your Sun sign is not important. If you want to know the true compatibility between two people, the easiest way is to study their charts together. To do so, you must calculate both charts and compare each planet: Venus with Venus, Mars with Mars. In each sign, we've explored how compatible it is with others, and you can apply this exercise to each position in the chart.

Are an astrological chart and a birth chart the same thing?

The astrological chart is a map of the sky at any given time. The birth chart is the astrological chart at the time a person is born.

Have the Zodiac signs changed? Is Ophiuchus the new sign?

No, they have not changed. The signs are the same as always. Ophiuchus is one more constellation. The confusion dates from a few years back when a rumor circulated that NASA declared Ophiuchus a new Zodiac sign. In truth, NASA never said such a thing, and even if they did, their decisions don't affect astrology.

Why don't I identify with my sign?

You are much more than your Sun sign. Create your birth chart and write down each planet and sign, each house, and each aspect, then analyze what you identify with and what you don't.

I want to emphasize once again that astrology is a tool used since ancient times to understand the world and ourselves. It's a vast field of exploration.

I hope that I've been able to give you a general idea of what is most important, and that this book is a fun guide for those who want to get started in this exciting world.

I hope that your learning is only just beginning and that it's wonderful.

Carlota

CARLOTA SANTOS is an architecture student and illustrator living in Spain. In 2020, she began to share drawings on Instagram as @carlotydes on topics related to astrology, from her own perspective and with a touch of humor. Currently, with thousands of followers around the globe, Carlota Santos is a vibrant and unique voice in the astrology universe, teaching the subject matter in a visual way.

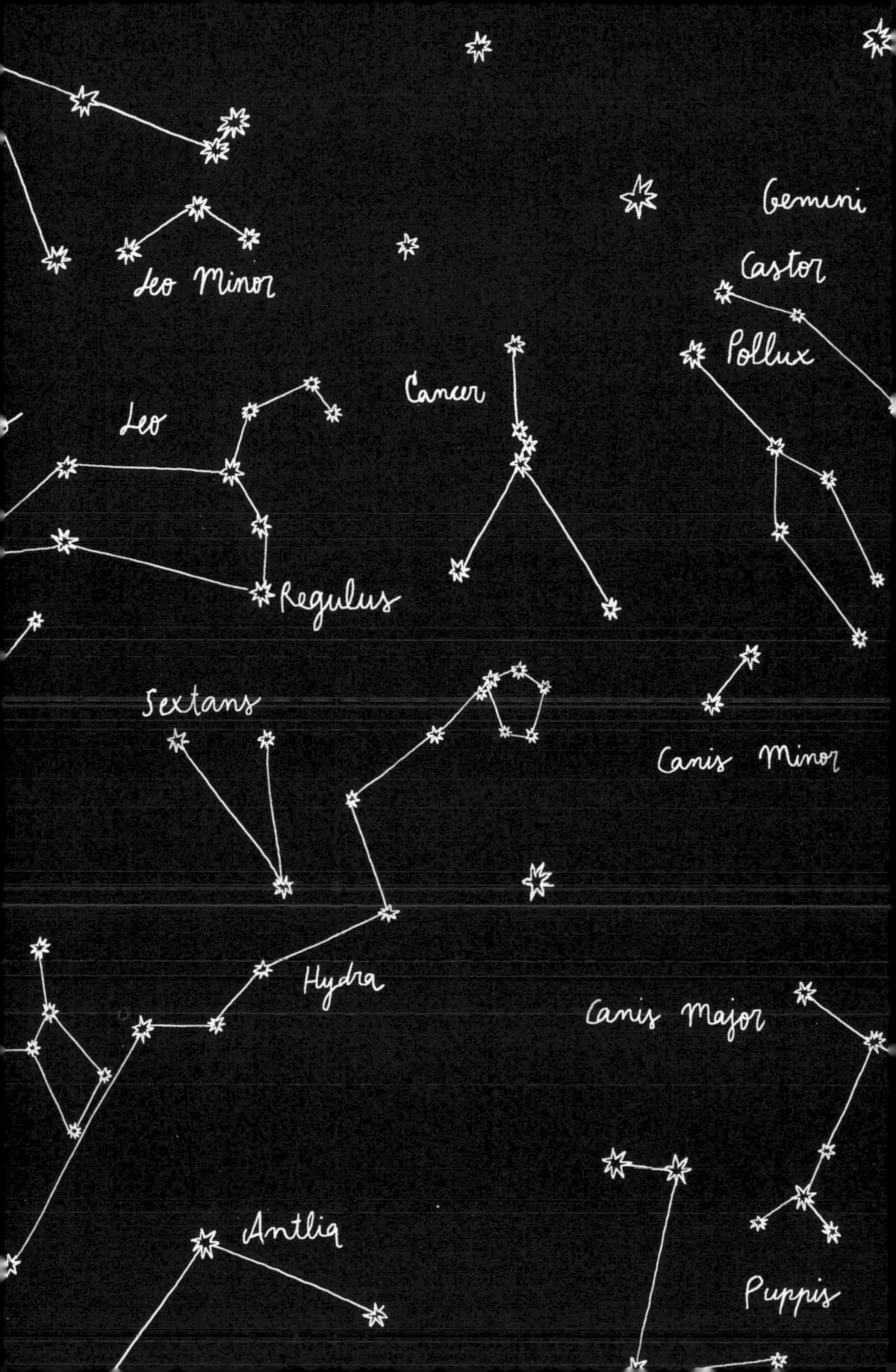

Leo Minor

Gemini

Castor

Pollux

Leo

Cancer

Regulus

Sextans

Canis Minor

Hydra

Canis Major

Antlia

Puppis

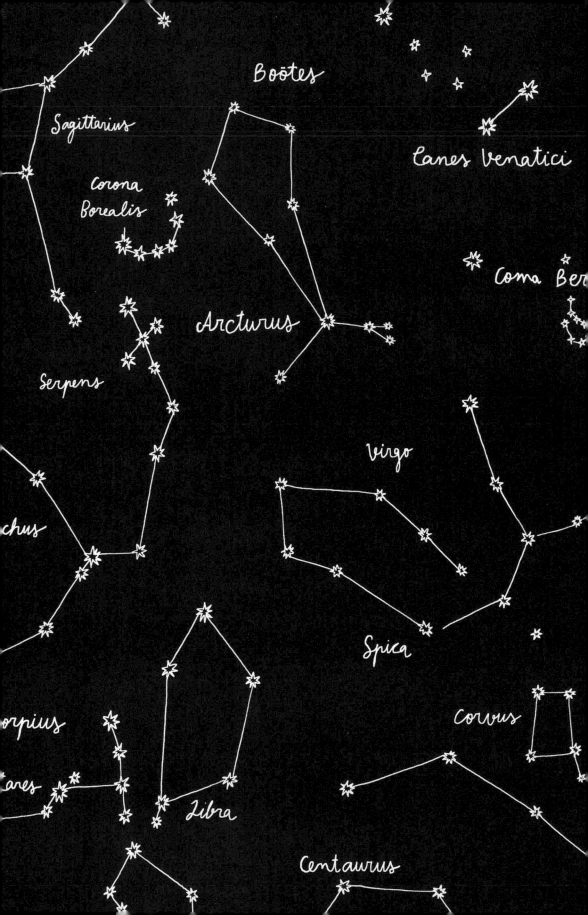

Boötes

Sagittarius

Canes Venatici

Corona
Borealis

Coma Ber

Arcturus

Serpens

Virgo

chus

Spica

rpius

Corvus

ares

Libra

Centaurus